THE OFFICIAL
11+
SERIES

THE OFFICIAL
PARENTS'
GUIDE TO THE 11+

Angus McDonald

GL
assessment
the measure of potential

Copyright © 2011 GL Assessment Limited

Published by GL Assessment Limited
389 Chiswick High Road, 9th Floor East, London, W4 4AL

www.gl-assessment.co.uk

GL Assessment is part of the Granada Learning Group

Designed by Starfish Design, Editorial and Project Management Ltd
Typeset by Mike Connor Design & Illustration
Cover photo © istockphoto.com/skodonnell

ISBN 978 0 7087 2056 1

1(4.11)

CONTENTS

PART 2 Supporting your child through the 11+

INTRODUCTION

Welcome to *The Official Parents' Guide to the 11+*. This book will help you prepare yourself and your child for the 11+ test, making it a positive experience.

The *Parents' Guide* is aimed at all parents and carers involved in the 11+ test, both those who are considering whether the 11+ test is right for their child and those who are already going through the 11+ process. Teachers and tutors will also find this book useful for background information and for extra ideas about 11+ test strategies.

For ease of reference, we use the term 'grammar schools' in this book, but other types of school are also selective – including independent schools, selective secondary schools and Local Authority-administered systems. All of these use selection tests, so this book will be relevant to parents of children applying to a wide range of selective schools.

The *Parents' Guide* starts with the basics about the 11+, giving you an understanding of the test itself and the test processes. It also explains how you can work with your child to help them prepare for the test in the best way possible. Although some readers may already be familiar with the 11+ test, or have received information from the school or Local Authority to which they are applying, this book starts from the beginning and assumes no prior knowledge of the 11+ test.

WHAT'S IN THE *PARENTS' GUIDE*?

This book is divided into two parts. Part 1 provides background information about the 11+ test and the test process, while Part 2 explores how you can support your child in developing their understanding of the 11+ test and the skills needed to complete it effectively.

PART 1: UNDERSTANDING THE 11+ AND HOW IT IS USED

Our research with parents tells us that one of their key concerns about the 11+ test is the lack of reliable information. The information provided by sources such as primary schools varies considerably in scope and depth, and it's often difficult to establish the credibility and accuracy of information from sources such as the internet. Part 1 of the *Parents' Guide* therefore provides parents with plenty of background information, to give you a greater understanding of the 11+ process and help you decide whether or not the 11+ is right for your child.

PART 2: SUPPORTING YOUR CHILD THROUGH THE 11+

Once you and your child have made a commitment to the 11+ test, your support and guidance will be essential to help your child prepare for the test itself. Part 2 therefore explores how you can support and work with your child through the 11+ test and make the experience positive.

HOW DO I USE THIS GUIDE?

Use this guide according to your specific needs – whether as a reference guide, focusing on the information that is relevant to you at a particular time, or by working through the book sequentially. Each chapter stands on its own, answering key questions about the 11+. As a whole, the book provides a comprehensive overview of the 11+ test and how to approach it.

The *Parents' Guide* provides:

- an authoritative source of information about the 11+, including the test itself and the processes around it
- guidance on developing a structured and motivating preparation programme for your child
- an overview of the types of question your child may encounter

- guidance on how to support your child's developing skills in answering the question types successfully
- advice on developing your child's test technique.

The table below indicates which chapters will be most useful at different stages of preparation.

Stage of preparation	Relevant chapters
Deciding whether to take the 11+ test	1, 2, 3, 4
Preparing your child for the 11+ test	5, 6, 9, 10, 11, 12, 13
Immediately before the 11+ test and the test itself	13
After the 11+ test	7, 8, 14

WORKING WITH YOUR CHILD

This feature highlights ideas and tips for activities that, as a parent or carer, you can do with your child to help their learning and development.

TRANSFERRABLE SKILLS

While the *Official 11+ Series* resources are designed specifically around the demands of the 11+ test, many of the skills that your child will learn by preparing for the test are relevant to other areas of their schooling and beyond – these are often called 'transferrable skills'. These include learning new ways of thinking and problem-solving, both of which are important for success in education and at work. Your child may also gain experience of multiple-choice tests and will develop test techniques, which they can apply to other tests. Throughout this book, we have highlighted 'transferrable skills'.

WHY CHOOSE GL ASSESSMENT?

In developing *The Official Parents' Guide to the 11+*, GL Assessment has drawn on its unrivalled expertise as providers of the majority of actual 11+ tests taken by children and over 30 years' experience in educational assessment. This allows us to present an authentic and balanced view of the test, how it works, the demands and requirements it places on children, and how it's used within selection systems. It also enables us to address the questions that parents most frequently ask about the 11+ tests.

The GL Assessment *Official 11+ Series*

The *Parents' Guide* is one of a series of *Official 11+* preparation materials published by GL Assessment. Each resource can be used on its own or with other titles in the series to provide comprehensive support for 11+ preparation.

The *11+ Explained* books for *Non-Verbal Reasoning* and *Verbal Reasoning* help your child develop their skills in these new areas, supported by tips, practice and essential strategies for improving their test technique.

11+ Practice Papers: Packs 1 and 2 for English, Maths, Non-Verbal Reasoning and Verbal Reasoning provide plenty of practice opportunities.

www.officialelevenplus.co.uk is a dedicated 11+ website offering further information and advice for parents, and digital practice tests.

IS THE 11+ RIGHT FOR MY CHILD?

The 11+ test is used because it assesses some of the cognitive abilities that are important for success in schooling and future life. The test is intentionally designed to challenge children and so there will always be some children who do well and some who do less well in the tests. It's only through this 'spreading children out' that the 11+ is of use to schools in their decision-making. Therefore, the nature of the selective test system means that any school using the 11+ test will offer places to only a small proportion of those who apply.

We recognise the importance of the 11+ test to both you and your child. The decision as to whether your child takes the 11+ should be made only after careful consideration, and your child should be involved in this decision. There are many points to consider when selecting the 'right' school for your child, and the right school won't necessarily be one that uses the 11+. Some factors that you may want to consider when deciding on whether to enter your child for the 11+ are discussed in Chapter 3.

PART 1

Understanding the 11+ and
how it is used

WHAT IS THE 11+?

The 11+ is a test used by some schools and Local Authorities in the UK as part of their selection procedures.

It was first introduced in 1944 when state-funded education in the UK was organised into grammar schools, secondary modern schools and secondary technical schools. In the UK and other parts of Europe, there was a strong belief that testing was a useful way of identifying a child's suitability for placement into different types of education, and so the 11+ was used to stream children into grammar, secondary modern or technical schools.

Changes in the education system over subsequent decades resulted in the 11+ largely being phased out, with the rise of comprehensive education during the 1970s. Although schools were banned from selecting on the basis of ability by the 1976 Education Act, they were again permitted to do this by the 1979 Education Act. Currently there are around 160 grammar schools in England that use the 11+ test and around 70 in Northern Ireland, plus many other selective secondary and independent schools across the UK.

THE NAME OF THE '11+ TEST'

The test that you and your child are preparing for is commonly known as the '11+' (or 'Eleven Plus'). This name dates back over 60 years, to when this type of test was first introduced. The 11+ takes its name from the age of entering secondary school, which is generally at 11 to 12 years old.

Some schools may use more modern names such as 'selection tests', 'entrance tests' or 'admissions tests', but they are referring to the same test.

In this book we use the term '11+' or '11+ test', as this is still widely used.

WHEN IS THE 11+ TAKEN?

Although the 11+ is no longer taken by every child, selective tests continue to be used by some schools and Local Authorities as part of the transition from primary to secondary education. The 11+ is usually taken by children when they are 10 or 11 years old, early in the academic year before they start secondary school. In a few cases entry into selective schools takes place at a different age, but this book will still be relevant.

WHY DO SCHOOLS USE THE 11+?

Schools use the 11+ for two reasons.

- First, demand for places in selective secondary schools is greater than the number of places available, so some form of selection is necessary. Schools therefore establish selection criteria that include a range of factors such as catchment area, siblings at the school and performance in the 11+.
- Second, schools use the 11+ to select children who are most likely to benefit from the style of education or specialisms offered by the school.

Schools find it very helpful to know about children's ability in a test like the 11+ as it provides a good predictor of their ability to learn, particularly in the more academic subjects that are often emphasised in selective schools.

11+ tests are designed to identify specific cognitive abilities that are essential for learning in the classroom. Such abilities depend far less on a child's previous educational experiences than Key Stage tests or GCSEs, though outcomes on these will be influenced by a child's underlying abilities. Most of the abilities covered by the 11+ are not taught directly in the classroom, as they are skills that underlie the development of knowledge that is part of the school curriculum. As most school assessment is focused on the curriculum, this also means that the abilities covered by the 11+ are not directly assessed through children's class work or many of the curriculum-based tests that they take.

Children displaying these particular types of abilities have been shown to thrive in the academically focused education offered by selective schools. Therefore, the 11+ is an important tool in matching children to the schools that will be most suitable for them.

The 11+ also offers a 'level playing field' as all children applying to a particular school take the same test, thus giving each child an equal opportunity to demonstrate their ability. This means that factors such as family background or which primary school a child attended don't influence selective secondary school entrance.

Children's results are reported relative to those of their peers, so schools are able to identify the most able children from their pool of applicants each year. 11+ tests are carefully designed and developed to provide a highly accurate measure of the capability they are assessing – they must have high 'reliability', to use the technical term. The scores therefore offer a precise indicator of your child's ability in the area measured by the test.

I HAVE HEARD OF THE 'COMMON ENTRANCE EXAM' – WHAT IS IT?

The Common Entrance exam is used by independent senior schools as part of their selection procedure, for entry at 11+ or 13+. Unlike the 11+ tests, the Common Entrance exam often requires children to produce extended answers and written exercises, and is based on published syllabuses. Common Entrance tests cover a range of curriculum areas including English, maths, science, classics, geography, history and modern languages.

Common Entrance tests are set by the Independent Schools Examination Board (ISEB). More information about these tests can be found at *www.iseb.co.uk*.

WHAT DOES THE 11+ MEASURE?

The 11+ test may consist of a single test or a series of tests, covering one or more of the following subjects:

- English
- Maths
- Non-Verbal Reasoning
- Verbal Reasoning

Which tests will my child take?

The Local Authority or individual school determines which subjects to test and the balance of question types within the tests. This means that the tests children take will vary across different schools and Local Authorities.

Children may take just one test in one subject area, multiple tests across more than one subject area, or multiple tests across all subject areas. Most 11+ tests will consist of a Verbal Reasoning test and many will also have a Non-Verbal Reasoning test. However, English and Maths tests are less frequently used as these subjects are more familiar to children and are more curriculum dependent.

For an up-to-date overview of the tests that make up the 11+ tests for each school or Local Authority, look at GL Assessment's 11+ website: *www.officialelevenplus.co.uk.*

It is also vital that you check these details directly with the school or Local Authority administering the process and refer to the information supplied directly by them at all times.

What are the tests like?

The English and Maths tests are based mainly around curriculum content reached within the early part of Year 6 (Northern Ireland P7). However, questions are likely to be more challenging than children are typically used to and also focus on your child's skills in these areas as much as their existing knowledge. The skills tested will therefore seem familiar to children, as will the type of tests used to assess these abilities, owing to their similarity with other curriculum-based tests, most notably the Key Stage tests.

Children are less likely to be familiar with Verbal and Non-Verbal Reasoning skills, although they may have taken other Verbal or Non-Verbal Reasoning tests at school, for example the *Cognitive Abilities Test*. For this reason, and because these core abilities are assessed by many 11+ tests, many resources such as GL Assessment's *11+ Explained* series focus on these skills.

There are 22 different question types that are generally used for the Verbal Reasoning test and 8 different question types for the Non-Verbal Reasoning test. Not all of these question types will necessarily appear in a single test paper.

We will introduce you to examples of some of the Verbal and Non-Verbal Reasoning question types in Chapter 2 and the Appendix. More detailed explanation and practice of each question type for Verbal and Non-Verbal Reasoning is provided in GL Assessment's *11+ Explained* series that complements this book.

HOW IS THE 11+ USED BY SCHOOLS IN THEIR SELECTION PROCESS?

Each admissions authority sets out its own criteria for selection in line with the Department for Education's Code of Admissions (*www.education.gov.uk/schools/adminandfinance/schooladmissions*). Selective schools and Local Authorities publish their admissions procedures, setting out how they decide which children will be accepted. These vary greatly across the country.

The 11+ test itself is often only one of several criteria that each child must meet in order to be considered. For example, children might not be permitted to take tests at some selective schools unless they live within a certain catchment area for the school.

As it's outside of the scope of this book to define each individual admissions authority's procedure, it's essential that you check these details directly with the school or Local Authority and always refer to the information supplied by them.

- ● WHY IS VERBAL REASONING IMPORTANT?
- ● WHAT IS THE VERBAL REASONING TEST LIKE?
- ● WHY IS NON-VERBAL REASONING IMPORTANT?
- ● WHAT IS THE NON-VERBAL REASONING TEST LIKE?
- ● WHAT IS THE MATHS TEST LIKE?
- ● WHAT IS THE ENGLISH TEST LIKE?
- ● CAN YOU TELL ME MORE ABOUT MULTIPLE-CHOICE TESTS?
- ● WHY ARE 11+ TESTS DESIGNED TO BE SO CHALLENGING?

WHY IS VERBAL REASONING IMPORTANT?

Verbal Reasoning tests identify the ability to think logically about written information and then to use it to solve problems. The keys to success include a good vocabulary and an ability to work logically with verbal information.

While the focus of Verbal Reasoning tests is mostly verbal, some questions also use numbers and can require basic numerical calculations to solve problems. Despite this, the underlying aspects being tested relate to Verbal Reasoning.

Much of our education system is verbally based, with a substantial amount of the content for all subjects being presented in written and spoken form. Verbal ability is therefore considered an important factor that will allow individuals to benefit from educational opportunities. For this reason, the most widely used 11+ test is Verbal Reasoning.

WHAT IS THE VERBAL REASONING TEST LIKE?

The Verbal Reasoning tests can be in standard or multiple-choice format. In standard format, the child is required to supply their answers independently, whereas in multiple-choice format the child identifies the correct answer from the answer options provided and marks it on the answer sheet. The multiple-choice format is the most commonly used and an example of the answer sheet is shown below.

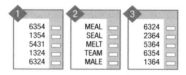 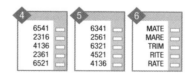 

Twenty-two types of question can appear in Verbal Reasoning tests. We have categorised these into the following groups:

- ● Cracking Codes
- ● Using Numbers
- ● Thinking Logically
- ● Creating Words
- ● Finding Words

Here, we'll show you an example of a question type from each category, as an introduction to what your child may encounter in the test. Examples of all 22 Verbal Reasoning question types are given in the Appendix. Take time to read through these, so that you get an idea of the nature of the test.

For detailed, step-by-step guidance on how to approach each of the 22 Verbal Reasoning question types, plus practice questions and strategies to develop your child's test technique, see GL Assessment's *11+ Explained – Verbal Reasoning* book.

CRACKING CODES: **Complete the Letter Series**

A B C D E F G H I J K L M N O P Q R S T U V W X Y Z
The alphabet is here to help you with these
questions. Find the next letters in the series
and mark the correct answer on the answer sheet.

Example

> CQ   DQ   EP   FP   (?)

Answer

> GO

CREATING WORDS: **Create a Compound Word**

In these questions, find **two** words, **one** from each group, that together make **one** correctly spelt word, without changing the order of the letters. The word from the first group always comes first. Mark **both** words on the answer sheet.

Example

> (out   by   open)
> (bite   like   side)

Answer

> **out**   **side** (The word is **outside**.)

USING NUMBERS: **Find the Number to Complete the Sum**

In each question, find the number that will complete the sum correctly and mark it on the answer sheet.

Example

> $3 + 5 = 6 + [?]$

Answer

> 2

FINDING WORDS: Find the Hidden Four-Letter Word

In these sentences, a word of **four letters** is hidden at the **end** of one word and the **beginning** of the next word. Find the pair of words that contains the hidden word and mark this answer on the answer sheet.

Example

The film ended happily after all.

Answer

film ended (The hidden word is **mend**.)

THINKING LOGICALLY: True or False

Read the following information, then find the correct answer to the question and mark it on the answer sheet.

Example

The children in the Jones family are called Archie, Jack, Charlie, Lucy and Emily.
Lucy is 1 year younger than Charlie.
Jack and Charlie are twins.
Archie is 3 years older than Lucy.
Jack is 8 years old.
Emily is older than Charlie, but younger than Archie.

If these statements are true, only one of the sentences below **must** be true.

Which one?

A   Emily is 11.

B   Archie is 2 years older than Emily.

C   All the children are younger than 10.

D   The sum of their ages is 45.

E   Archie is 10.

Answer

E

TRANSFERRABLE SKILLS

Verbal Reasoning is an important skill that will help your child in their education and beyond by encouraging them to:

● develop literacy and vocabulary skills
● think critically about written information
● deal more confidently with new written material.

WHY IS NON-VERBAL REASONING IMPORTANT?

Non-Verbal Reasoning tests identify the ability to solve problems using pictures and shapes. The keys to success include the ability to think analytically, come up with new ideas about how to solve problems and spot patterns and relationships between shapes.

As Non-Verbal Reasoning tests don't require the use of language, and the problem-solving tasks they involve are quite different from the skills children generally develop through their education, they are seen by psychologists as one of the 'purest' means of testing ability.

Moreover, as Non-Verbal Reasoning does not rely on high levels of language ability, performance in these tests is also less influenced by fluency in English. Non-Verbal Reasoning tests are therefore a good indicator of potential in children irrespective of their verbal ability. The use of pictures and shapes also means that Non-Verbal Reasoning tests can assess an individual's ability to deal with unfamiliar information and to acquire new ideas and concepts.

WHAT IS THE NON-VERBAL REASONING TEST LIKE?

Non-Verbal Reasoning tests require candidates to identify the correct answer from those provided. Non-Verbal Reasoning tests are multiple-choice. While some Non-Verbal Reasoning tests are called standard format, in this case it means that children write their answer in the test booklet, rather than using a separate answer sheet.

Eight types of question can appear in Non-Verbal Reasoning tests. We have categorised these into the following groups:

- Finding Similarities and Differences
- Completing Diagrams
- Cracking Codes

We have included an example of a question type from each of these categories below. Examples of all eight Non-Verbal Reasoning question types are given the Appendix.

FINDING SIMILARITIES AND DIFFERENCES: **Find the Diagram Like the First Three**

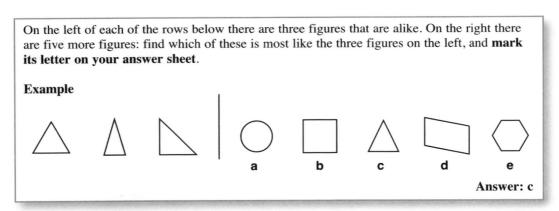

In this example, all the diagrams on the left are triangles with three sides. Therefore, **c** is the correct answer as it is the only one of the five diagrams that is a triangle.

COMPLETING DIAGRAMS: **Complete the Grid**

In the big square on the left of each line below one of the small squares has been left empty. One of the five figures on the right should fill the empty square. Find this figure and **mark its letter on your answer sheet**.

Example

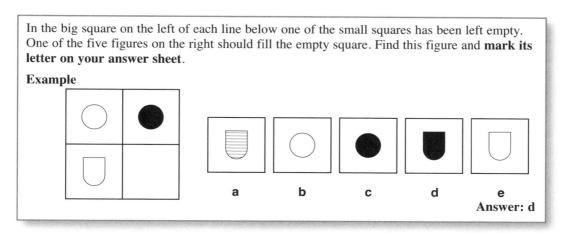

Answer: **d**

In the example above the two shapes at the top are both the same, except that the circle on the left is white and the one on the right is black. In the bottom left, there is a white shield shape. To complete the pattern, the missing shape has to be a shield that is shaded black, so the correct answer must be **d**.

CRACKING CODES: **Crack the Horizontal Code**

To answer these questions you have to work out a code. In the boxes on the left are shapes and the code letters that go with them. The top letters mean something different to the bottom ones. You must decide how the letters go with the shapes. Then find the correct code for the **test shape** from the set of five codes on the right. **Mark its letter on your answer sheet.**

Look at **Example 1**:

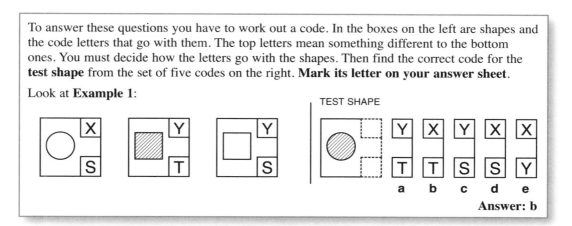

Answer: **b**

In the example above, two of the top letters are the same (Y) and one is different (X). Two of the bottom three letters are also the same (S) and one is different (T). The top letters will therefore describe a feature that is shared between the second and third diagrams but is different from the first – in this example this is the shape, as the first shape is a circle and the second and third are squares.

The bottom letters must describe a feature that is common to the first and third diagrams, but different from the second. In this case the letters must relate to the shading, as the first and third shapes are not shaded whereas the middle shape is shaded with diagonal lines. The test diagram is a shaded circle. The code for circle is 'X' and for a shaded shape is 'T'. The answer is therefore **b**.

WORKING WITH YOUR CHILD

For detailed, step-by-step guidance on how to approach each of the eight Non-Verbal Reasoning question types, plus practice questions and strategies to develop your child's test technique, refer to GL Assessment's *11+ Explained – Non-Verbal Reasoning* book.

WHAT IS THE MATHS TEST LIKE?

Maths tests are more familiar to us. They tend to be used by selective schools that are particularly interested in technical areas such as maths, technology, science and engineering. They also give an indication of a child's attainment level in maths to date. For this reason, they are often used in conjunction with a Verbal Reasoning test, a Non-Verbal Reasoning test, or both, to highlight children who are possibly more able than their previous educational experience has allowed them to reach and demonstrate in this key area of education.

The 11+ Maths tests follow the curriculum and cover topics that children will have covered naturally at school by the beginning of Year 6 (P7). Even so, some questions in the 11+ tests will be based on concepts taught in the classroom but will be at a more difficult level than all children will have covered in primary school.

The Maths tests can be in standard or multiple-choice format. In standard format the child is required to supply their answers independently, whereas in multiple-choice format the child identifies the correct answer from the answer options provided and marks it on the answer sheet. The multiple-choice format is the most commonly used.

WHAT IS THE ENGLISH TEST LIKE?

Again, English tests are more familiar to us. They are used by selective schools that are particularly interested in areas such as English, history, languages and literature. They also give an indication of a child's attainment level in English to date. Like the 11+ Maths tests, they are therefore often used with a Verbal Reasoning test, a Non-Verbal Reasoning test, or both, to highlight children who may be more able than they have been able to demonstrate so far in this key area.

The tests take the form of a number of passages that must be read in order to answer a set of questions. These questions will cover passage comprehension, sentence completion, grammar, spelling, word meanings, and understanding of common book-related terms and their purpose (for example, glossary). The English tests are multiple-choice format.

CAN YOU TELL ME MORE ABOUT MULTIPLE-CHOICE TESTS?

Multiple-choice questions are used extensively in 11+ exams, but your child may not be familiar with them. For each question, your child will be presented with a series of answer options, one of which is correct while the others are all incorrect. They have to decide which of the answer options is correct and then indicate this on their answer sheet.

WORKING WITH YOUR CHILD

Here are some tips that will help your child with multiple-choice questions:

- Multiple-choice answer sheets leave quite small spaces for answers, so it's very important to be accurate when selecting the answers.
- As your child will need to switch between their question paper and answer sheet frequently, they should keep checking that they are marking their answers in the correct place. Placing both close together on their desk will help minimise any errors.
- If they do skip a question, they must leave the corresponding space on their answer sheet.
- If your child gives the same answer to a number of consecutive questions, this shouldn't lead them to automatically question whether they are right. It's quite possible for the correct answer option for three or even four questions in a row to have the same letter.
- The correct answer will always be one of the options given so, if your child finds a question particularly difficult, encourage them to try to eliminate some answers that they are sure are wrong and then to make their best guess from those remaining.
- Answer sheets are marked by machine, so your child must only use pencil and should make sure that any changed answers are rubbed out properly.

WHY ARE 11+ TESTS DESIGNED TO BE SO CHALLENGING?

Children may find the 11+ tests challenging. It's also common for parents to find some questions quite challenging when they first look at them. There are two main reasons for this.

First, as already emphasised, children are likely to have little if any experience of this type of Verbal and Non-Verbal Reasoning test. As with anything new, we will typically find it difficult when we first try it and think there is a lot to learn. But, with experience, we don't always remember why we thought it would be so challenging. Think about learning to drive a car and how much there was to learn at first. Remember, although parts of the 11+ may seem difficult at first, this does not mean they won't become easier as your child becomes familiar with them and learns how to approach the test effectively. For all these reasons, it is recommended that you help your child prepare and become familiar with the tests.

Second, although familiarity is important, the tests are also designed to be challenging. As discussed above, schools use the tests to help them differentiate between many able children. To do this effectively, the tests need to be able to stretch even the most able minds!

IS THE 11+ RIGHT FOR MY CHILD?

- **HOW SHOULD I INVOLVE MY CHILD IN THE DECISION?**
- **WHAT ISSUES SHOULD I CONSIDER WHEN ENTERING MY CHILD FOR THE 11+ TEST?**
- **WHAT ELSE SHOULD I FIND OUT?**
- **HOW DO I BRING ALL THE INFORMATION TOGETHER TO MAKE A DECISION?**

HOW SHOULD I INVOLVE MY CHILD IN THE DECISION?

Involving your child in all the decisions around the 11+ test is one of the key messages that we promote throughout this *Parents' Guide*. It's crucial for getting your child's 'buy-in' and motivation for preparation.

Involving your child can be difficult, especially when parents and children have different views. Nevertheless, there are a number of significant benefits in involving your child in the decision-making.

One of the most tricky situations to deal with is when parents and child have very different opinions about school choice and, therefore, whether to take the 11+ or not. We will provide some ideas on how to cope with this later in this chapter.

Benefits of involving your child in decisions

- It lets them know that their opinions and ideas count and that they are being listened to and taken seriously.
- The process will enable you to acknowledge their concerns and anxieties about the 11+ test and their transition to a new school, more generally.
- Your child will have unique insights into their situation. It's sometimes tempting to think that our experience as parents means that we understand situations better than our children do and so are more able to make the right decisions. But we don't always know exactly how our children think and feel about the important events in their lives. Try to see things from their perspective so that you can make a more informed decision.
- Finally, and most importantly, involving your child in the decision will give them a sense of ownership of the final decision you make together. This, in turn, will lead to their motivation in whatever decision is made – whether this is working towards the 11+ or looking forward to making a success of their time at a non-selective school. Motivation will almost certainly be lacking if they are just presented with the decision.

WORKING WITH YOUR CHILD

When working with your child to make the decision about whether or not to take the 11+, it's essential to be patient and to discuss all the options. Try not to rush to a decision too quickly. Also try not to let the discussion become too emotional; try to consider all possibilities rationally and clearly. Encourage your child to be open about how they are feeling and accept that there are no 'right' or 'wrong' decisions. Working together in this way will encourage shared commitment to whatever decision you reach together.

Ways to involve your child

There is no 'right' way to involve your child in the decision-making process for the 11+. How you go about making the decision will inevitably be influenced by the dynamics of the relationships within your family, but you should approach this decision in the same way as you would any other situation where people have to reach a joint decision.

- Set aside some time to discuss the decision with your child. They may want to think about the 11+ on their own before you talk about it with them, so give them a few days to do this.
- Make sure that you both know the purpose of the discussion. This may sound obvious, but don't assume that you have a clearly shared purpose.
- Don't expect to arrive at an answer quickly. Either or both of you may need time to go away and think about your decision, otherwise you may be unhappy with it later on.
- Encourage your child to think about different views and issues that they haven't considered (for example, the impact of the decision on their educational opportunities). These may not necessarily be your own views, but the more issues you can consider at this point, the less likely it is that different views will crop up in the future to challenge your decision.
- It's easy to focus on the immediate decision, but you may need to encourage your child to consider the longer-term picture by helping them to grasp the impact this decision may have on their future.
- Try not to simply present your child with your own views. Instead, prompt your child to think about the implications of choosing to take the 11+ on their future education and beyond. Putting forward your views too soon can put pressure on your child, even if you don't mean to.
- If you feel anxious about the 11+ and its implications, or have strong views about the different options, be aware of these and try not to overly influence your child.
- Listen to your child at all times and try to understand their position. Try not to judge or contradict their views if they are different from yours; while your child may not have as much experience as you, this does not mean that their views are any less valid.

TRANSFERRABLE SKILLS

When deciding whether to take the 11+ or not, your child is developing their skills in working collaboratively, sharing information and opinions, and reaching a conclusion. Working effectively with others is one of the skills most highly valued by employers.

WHAT ISSUES SHOULD I CONSIDER WHEN ENTERING MY CHILD FOR THE 11+ TEST?

Depending on your Local Authority or school, your child may be automatically entered for the 11+ test or you may have to enter them for it. If your child is at a school where they are entered automatically for the 11+, you will probably be aware of this and may already have been contacted by the school and given details about the test. It is possible to opt out of the test, should you wish to, but make sure that you consider your decision carefully. If your school does not automatically enter children for the 11+ test, which is likely to be the case if you are applying to a secondary school outside your area, you will need to contact the secondary school or its Local Authority directly to find out what you need to do to enter your child. However, even if pupils are entered automatically for the 11+, it may still be possible to opt out of it.

Whether this leaves you with the decision to 'opt in' or to 'opt out' of the 11+ test, either choice is likely to be a significant decision for your child and family. For some, this decision may come easily. For others, it won't be so easy as there are several important factors to consider:

11+ opportunities

The 11+ offers your child a great opportunity to learn many new skills, whether they gain entrance to a selective school or not. Throughout this book we have highlighted 'transferrable skills'. These illustrate key skills that your child will develop when working towards their 11+, which can be applied to other areas of their education and beyond. Many other valuable learning opportunities accompany the preparation process, such as planning, self-motivation and working with others.

All children should be encouraged to feel a great sense of achievement when they have completed the 11+, regardless of the outcome.

11+ challenge

The purpose of the 11+ is to help schools select the most able pupils, so it's designed to be challenging, to 'discriminate' between pupils, many of whom will be very able. You and your child therefore need to consider carefully whether taking the 11+ is really right for them. To do this, we recommend that you look at evidence from a number of sources to check whether their abilities are suited to the academic challenge of the 11+. Ability should be one of the main factors that you consider when deciding whether to enter them for the 11+. Evidence of ability can come from a number of sources:

- tests your child has taken at school (for example SATs, subject-specific tests and standardised tests such as the *Cognitive Abilities Test*)
- teacher assessments and reports of their academic progress
- your evaluation and your child's evaluation of their capabilities, not in formal terms but more about how confident they feel with different subjects and the progress that they have recently been making at school.

Your child's teacher will also be a valuable source of information both on broader aspects about your child, such as their motivation, and on possible schools. It's therefore a good idea to discuss your child's options with their teacher before making a decision.

It's also worth finding out what specific tests will be used within the 11+ in your area and looking at your child's academic results in these subjects where possible. Where they are used, the Maths and English tests are very similar in content to standard curriculum assessments, although they will include an added 'challenge' in terms of their level of difficulty, to reflect their use as selection tests. Your child's attainment in Maths and English can therefore offer a good indicator of their likely performance in the corresponding 11+ tests.

The Verbal and Non-Verbal Reasoning tests are quite different from curriculum-based tests that your child is likely to have taken, meaning that it will be difficult to make direct inferences from academic results. If your child has taken the *Cognitive Abilities Test*, which contains Verbal and Non-Verbal Reasoning sections, high scores in this will be a good indicator that your child is likely to perform at least reasonably well in the 11+ tests. However, note that there are significant differences between the tests, particularly that the 11+ is designed to be much more challenging.

11+ competition

The purpose of the 11+ is to select between large numbers of pupils, as there are not enough places to meet the demand. In recent years, competition has increased – some areas of England have seen more than a 15% increase in the number of children taking the 11+ since 2009. One of the main reasons for the recent increase in applications is that parents who might previously have sent their children to independent schools are now looking at grammar schools in order to save on school fees.

Increased competition makes it even more important that children are as well prepared as they can be, so that they can demonstrate their true potential through the 11+ tests.

11+ commitment

No set commitment is required of children who take the 11+ test, but it's very likely that parents will expect their children to do some preparation for the test. Schools may also offer children the opportunity to do some preparation.

Each parent will differ in the amount of preparation they will expect from their child – everything from minimal preparation shortly before the test to intensive preparation starting a long time in advance. It's usual that preparation for the test extends over at least six months and maybe up to a year. Some children may spend longer than this, but we do not consider this necessary or even, in some cases, beneficial.

The time children spend on 11+ preparation each week might also vary from around 30 minutes up to a few hours, but will be partly dependent on how long before the test children begin their preparation. As a general rule, short practice sessions of around 30 minutes to an hour, spread out over a period of time, will be best for most children. Short sessions will be more motivating for your child and doing smaller, 'bite-size' bits of preparation, during which they are more likely to remained focused, gives them a greater chance of retaining the learning.

For your child's 11+ test results to be a true reflection of their ability, both you and your child need to be fully committed to the 11+ and motivated to give the necessary time and effort to prepare appropriately.

WHAT ELSE SHOULD I FIND OUT?

Having looked at opportunity, challenge, competition and commitment when deciding whether the 11+ is right for your child, there are many other issues to consider.

It's always a challenge to separate out facts, feelings and opinions when making important decisions. One way to overcome this is to use a structured approach to gather all the information you need about the 11+ and then consider the benefits and issues associated with different decisions. The headings and questions below will help you do this.

Do you know all the facts?

- Have you found out everything you need to about the 11+ test and the application process?
- Have you identified all the possible schools in you area, then decided on those which you want to consider further and those that you don't?
- Have you found out about all the schools that you are thinking of applying to (for example, by looking at their prospectuses)?
- Have you thought carefully about your child – their character, wishes and peer group?
- Is there anything else that you need to consider, such as family circumstances?

What options are open to you?

- Have you thought about both selective and non-selective schools?
- Are there any other schools or education options for your child that you have not considered?
- Can you apply to a number of schools, possibly some that are selective and others that are not?

Have you evaluated all the options fully?

- Have you thought carefully about all the options, rather than dismissing some without careful consideration?
- Have your evaluations been logical, rather than being guided mainly by your feelings?
- Have you considered all the aspects referred to in this chapter and any others relevant to you (for example, the school environment and ethos, transport arrangements and opportunities for your child to pursue special interests, as well as their ability)?

Have you fully considered the impact on all those involved?

- Your child?
- Immediate family?
- Any other relatives or anyone else who needs to be considered?

There may also be other questions you want to add under these headings. Using these headings will enable you to be more systematic in your decision-making, so that the final decision is best for your child.

HOW DO I BRING ALL THE INFORMATION TOGETHER TO MAKE A DECISION?

If you have answered all the questions above you will probably have gathered a lot of information. Now you need to use this to make the decision about whether or not to enter your child for the 11+ test.

> **TRANSFERRABLE SKILLS**
>
> Supporting your child to identify all the different information that needs to be considered when deciding whether to take the 11+, and then encouraging them to bring this together to make a final decision, helps them develop very valuable information-collecting and decision-making skills.

Your child and the school – a good fit?

This table shows you one way to bring together all of the information, thoughts and feelings to make this decision. The idea of 'fit' is a useful way to think about the schools that are likely to be best suited to your child. It tries to compare all the things that are important to you and your child with features of the schools you are considering (whether selective or otherwise) to see how good the match is.

Your child	Feature of schools under consideration
Your child's ability as indicated by their school reports, achievement in tests, their teachers' evaluations, and your own and your child's evaluations	How academically oriented is the school and what is its relative focus on academic achievement versus other elements of the curriculum (e.g. artistic activities) and extra-curricular activities? Do they have specialisms in certain areas of the curriculum?
Your child's character (e.g. are they outgoing, relaxed, conscientious and intellectually curious?)	What is the overall ethos of the school (e.g. how do children and staff relate to each other and what is the role of the school in the wider community)?
Your child's and your own views about the importance of siblings attending the same school	Do siblings attend the same school? Does the school give priority to siblings?
Your child's desire to remain with their current school friends	Are your child's friends also applying to the same school?
The balance of your child's interests between academic and more practical or creative interests	What opportunities does the school offer for pursuing practical and creative interests alongside academic ones? What extra-curricular activities are on offer?

Your child	Feature of schools under consideration
Your child's specific talents (e.g. musical or sporting) that they are keen to pursue	Is the school willing and able to support children in the development of specific talents and do they have the facilities to do this?
Other issues for your child – travelling to schools (e.g. availability of transport, time and affordability), impact on family life	What is the location of the school? Does it provide transport? Is public transport convenient and safe? How long will the journey take out of your child's day? Could you car share?

Schools that meet more of your requirements or are more closely matched to your child and their circumstances are likely to be a better 'fit'. Schools that fit more closely with your child's abilities, preferences, character and interests are more likely to provide an environment where they will be happy and successful. Your child is less likely to thrive in schools that are not such a good fit.

Finally ...

As a parent, it's only natural that you will have strong views about what's best for your child's education and encourage them accordingly. At times this will be very important, if they are to achieve their full potential. However, do consider the needs and views of your child as well as your own aspirations for them.

Be realistic in your appraisal of your child's abilities and how well suited these are to the usually highly academic orientation of selective schools. While you should value your child's ability and achievements, it won't benefit them to be over-optimistic and enter them for the 11+ test only to find that your child then struggles in a selective school even though they were successful in the test. Remember that this decision will affect the next five to seven years of their education, and maybe beyond, and that non-selective schools may provide an environment in which your child will thrive.

There are many successful paths that a child can take throughout their education. Some children will be very successful in a non-selective school that best meets their needs and allows them to express and develop their individual strengths, whereas others will flourish in selective schools.

NOT TAKING THE 11+?

If your decision is to not to enter your child for the 11+, this in no way implies 'failure'. If you have considered all the options and weighed the evidence carefully, and then decided not to take the 11+, then this will be the best decision for both you and your child.

- **HOW DO I START THE 11+ PROCESS AND SCHOOL APPLICATION?**
- **HOW DOES THE APPLICATION PROCESS WORK?**

HOW DO I START THE 11+ PROCESS AND SCHOOL APPLICATION?

Once you and your child have decided that you would like your child to take the 11+ test, the next step is to ensure that your child is enrolled with the selective school or Local Authority of your choice. In some areas, this may mean that you need to apply to a number of different places.

It's important to note that this application process may be separate from the admissions process within your Local Authority where you will indicate your child's preferred schools when applying to a new secondary school.

HOW DOES THE APPLICATION PROCESS WORK?

1 The first point of call should be to discuss the options and possibilities with your child's primary school. They will be able to provide you with accurate information on any Local Authority requirements, the steps you must take and any deadlines you must meet.

In some areas of the UK, the Local Authority will automatically enter your child for the 11+.

Your child's primary school will also be able to advise on specific secondary schools nearby and whether any use the 11+, together with information about the application process for each.

2 The second step is to get in touch directly with the schools to which you are interested in applying. They are likely to run open days that you can attend to help you decide on the right school and can provide the exact information you need to make your application, should you decide to do so. They will also be able to confirm the exact subject tests that your child will need to take; these may well be different for each school.

Each school's requirements and deadlines are likely to be different, so make sure that you plan enough time to research everything, complete and post the application forms and meet all the deadlines necessary. Though there may be some schools that you want to rule out early on in the decision-making process, there will probably be two or more that you want to give careful consideration to. Wait until you have all the information you need, so that you can consider all the options carefully.

The internet, in particular, is an important research tool, with many schools now providing very detailed and informative websites of their own. You can also find an up-to-date list of the tests that make up the 11+ tests for each school or Local Authority, on GL Assessment's 11+ website: *www.officialelevenplus.co.uk.*

It's imperative that you check all details directly with the school or Local Authority administering the process, too, and refer to the information supplied by them at all times.

- WHAT TYPES OF PREPARATION ARE THERE?
- SHOULD I LOOK FOR MORE SUPPORT TO HELP MY CHILD?
- WHY IS PREPARATION SO IMPORTANT?
- WHAT DOES RESEARCH TELL US ABOUT EFFECTIVE PREPARATION?
- SO WHAT NEXT?

WHAT TYPES OF PREPARATION ARE THERE?

If your child is going to take the 11+ test, you will want them to do the best they possibly can and so Part 2 will focus on how you can work directly with your child to support their preparation for the test.

Here we will consider some of the different activities that are often associated with preparing for the 11+ test, to help you decide what's right for *your* child. We'll also look at what the research tells us about effective preparation, to help guide your planning.

You will probably have come across these words in relation to the 11+, as they are commonly used to describe activities that help get children ready for taking the test. Even though they all have the same aim, each term can relate to quite different activities. Therefore, it's essential to understand what each involves so that you can decide what's best for *your* child. These terms are not precisely defined or always used consistently, but we will use them in this book to describe the following activities.

PREPARATION

Preparation is quite general and can cover any activity that you engage in to help your child get ready for the 11+ test. This could range from reading about what the test involves through to intensive practice and tutoring. All of the activities described below are examples of specific types of preparation.

FAMILIARISATION

Familiarisation also covers a broad range of activities, all of which are intended to help your child understand more about the 11+ and what it involves. Some schools or Local Authorities will offer your child practice tests. The reason for this is that the types of question used in the 11+, particularly in the Verbal and Non-Verbal Reasoning tests, are likely to be new to children. Familiarisation will give your child at least a basic understanding of the 11+, the types of questions that they will encounter and the presentation of the test booklets and answer sheets they will need to use.

PRACTICE

Practice refers to activities that involve your child taking 11+ test questions. This may be trying out the different types of test questions or taking complete practice tests. Practice may be untimed or timed to simulate test conditions. After your child has completed test questions, they should review them. This review may vary in depth – it might simply be scoring questions to see which they got right or wrong. Or it might involve looking through questions that they answered incorrectly to see where the problems lie and what needs to be practised further.

COACHING AND TUTORING

Coaching and tutoring probably arouse more debate and emotion than anything else related to the 11+. Coaching is likely to involve many of the activities described above, but is distinct from them in two key ways. First, children may work intensively with a tutor, either individually or in a group, attending coaching sessions over a period of time. Second, coaching will normally include a detailed focus on the individual question types that may be found in the 11+, and will train children in the use of specific approaches and strategies to solve each question type. It's also likely to cover more general approaches that are helpful in tackling the 11+ tests. Coaching is often provided by independent tutors or companies, usually operating on a commercial basis, many of whom claim that their courses lead to significant gains in test performance.

SHOULD I LOOK FOR MORE SUPPORT TO HELP MY CHILD?

At this point you may be thinking that you want to get further support to help your child prepare for their 11+. Just as the experience can be daunting for children, it can also seem overwhelming to parents.

If you are thinking about getting additional support, we would encourage you to:

- Read the rest of this book, then you will be able to make a more informed decision about the commitment needed from you and the nature of the support you may need to give your child.
- Look at resources such as the *11+ Explained* books and decide how much this type of information will allow you to provide the necessary support to your child.
- Consider your capacity to provide the support your child needs – do you have the time to do this?
- Are there aspects of your child's 11+ preparation where they may benefit from external input?
- Find out what support is available through your school, as they may be offering 11+ preparation classes.
- If you still want to seek additional help:
  - Get recommendations from friends or your child's school.
  - Check out the credentials of possible tutors – what makes them well-placed to help your child with the 11+?
  - Ask for references from parents of children whom they have tutored previously and follow these up.
  - Find out as much as you can about how they would help your child – the best preparation will cover a range of activities and not just intensive drilling with practice papers.
  - Ask a potential tutor about what they realistically expect to achieve; be wary of anyone claiming too much.
  - Think about whether the tutor is likely to be a match for your child, in terms of their style of working and find out about how flexible the support will be – will your child follow a standard programme or will it be tailored to their specific needs?
  - Finally, ensure that tutors have appropriate safeguarding checks in place.

Ultimately, the choice to seek additional support needs to be a joint decision between you and your child. Whatever decision you make, remember that there can be no guarantees in a competitive system such as the 11+.

WHY IS PREPARATION SO IMPORTANT?

All types of preparation activities aim to help children improve their scores in the 11+, but they all work in slightly different ways.

Why prepare?

The school or Local Authority that sets the 11+ is really interested in knowing about a child's *true* ability, so the point of the test is to measure this as accurately as possible.

You can see from the diagram opposite that ability, although essential for good 11+ performance, can be influenced by several other factors that affect test performance. Although ability is fundamental to performance, it is influenced by how much your child understands about the question type and the strategies they apply.

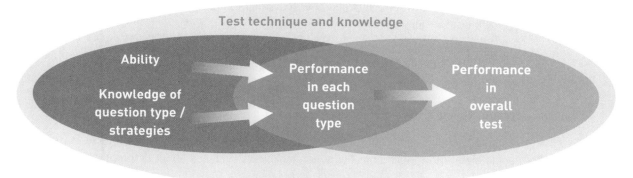

More intensive coaching activities often focus on systematically looking at all the possible question types a child may encounter, ensuring that they recognise each question type and know what type of answer is required, and giving them strategies and tips to answer it quickly and accurately. Understanding the question types and learning relevant strategies will help a to child to answer the question correctly, particularly under test conditions.

However, simple familiarisation activities, which can be done at home or may be organised by the school, will also help children learn how to answer the different question types. This is usually achieved through looking at sample questions and taking practice papers and this can often be done flexibly at home. Although the intensity of home tuition is likely to be less, with the right knowledge and motivation it can be just as effective as using external support.

How well a child performs on individual questions will obviously have a direct effect on how they perform in the test overall. The more questions that a child answers correctly, the higher their score will be. Practice with sets of questions or full tests can be particularly helpful here. Practice tests may be given by your child's primary school, or practice sessions may be offered by the school to which you are applying. They may be given under untimed or timed conditions. Timed practice is an effective way of helping children appreciate the demands of completing the 11+ under test conditions, where they will be required to maintain good speed throughout.

In the diagram above, you will see that test technique surrounds ability and performance. Test technique refers to anything a child does in the test situation that helps their performance. Test technique is a key 'enabler', helping a child bring together all the elements involved in successful performance and allowing their true ability to show through in the test.

In contrast, a child with poor test technique and less effective use of strategies for answering specific question types is likely to perform less well in the test than they should for their ability.

YOUR ROLE IN 11+ PREPARATION

We will explore test technique and knowledge in detail in Part 2 of the *Parents' Guide* so that you can see how best to help your child show their true ability. As a parent, you can provide activities and support for your child that will target all the key areas described here. Whichever type of preparation you decide is appropriate to meet your child's needs, you need to get to grips with the demands on your child and support them throughout the process.

WORKING WITH YOUR CHILD

GL Assessment's *Practice Papers* and *11+ Explained* books offer you and your child a comprehensive set of resources for preparation. Together these will enable you to support your child through a thorough preparation programme leading up to the 11+ itself.

WHAT DOES RESEARCH TELL US ABOUT EFFECTIVE PREPARATION?

Research consistently shows that preparation has an effect on test performance. What's less clear is what types of preparation are most effective and how they might impact on the different types of test that can form part of the 11+. Unfortunately, research on the 11+ is limited.

Here we will consider the available evidence to help guide you and your child on how best to use your time when preparing for the 11+.

What research is there?

The competitive and personally significant role of the 11+ in children's education undoubtedly makes it difficult for people always to remain objective when looking at evidence about different types of preparation.

Despite this, we shouldn't just take any claims about the effectiveness of different approaches to preparation at face value. We need to understand fully what's being offered by providers of test preparation resources and services. We should also try to assess the authenticity of their claims about the impact of their resources and services on a child's test performance.

Although research on the 11+ itself is limited, studies have been carried out on other tests that are used for academic selection. In many cases, the tests and the issues explored are similar to those in the 11+. Therefore, the results from these studies, together with research directly considering the 11+, can help us understand the effects of preparation on the 11+.

Finally, it's almost impossible to conduct proper scientific research around live tests such as the 11+, which have a significant impact on children's educational choices. For example, it would be unethical to assign children randomly to receive 'coaching' or 'no coaching' for the purpose of scientific research. Studies therefore have to rely on looking at people who have made the decision to receive coaching. The drawback is that this decision may have been influenced by a range of background factors that are also related to test performance. This means that it's difficult to draw clear and unambiguous conclusions from research, and findings can often be interpreted according to an individual's existing beliefs and motives.

Bearing all this in mind, the following section provides an outline of what we know about the effects of preparation.

What does the research tell us?

One piece of research investigates the effects of coaching on test scores. While the conclusions are not clear-cut, we will explore the research below.

Coaching versus the practice effect

The most common way in which the effect of coaching is demonstrated is to test people once, get them to go through a coaching course and then give them the same or a similar test again, as illustrated below. Scores in Test 1 are then compared with scores in Test 2, to see whether coaching has had an effect on test performance. This type of research often illustrates positive changes in score and is used to support the benefits of coaching.

But what happens if a child taking the two tests does not receive any coaching between the tests, as illustrated below? In this case, scores often change, too. This is often referred to as a 'practice effect' – that is, a change in score that results simply from gaining practice in the test.

Time

As would be expected, scores generally increase when a test is repeated. Scores can also increase slightly for children who have had coaching. However, before these results are taken as an endorsement of coaching, it's important to stress that:

- these results are 'on average' – that is, what we see when we look at the results from large groups of children
- although there are 'average' gains in test score, some children improve, some children stay the same and others achieve a lower test score when taking the test a second time.

Coaching does not always lead to higher scores
One of the most detailed studies on the effects of coaching looked at its effect on the American SAT entrance test for universities.

This study found large score gains in 12–16% of those who received coaching (depending on the type of SAT test studied), though this study adopted a very broad definition of 'coaching' as being any activity conducted outside of normal school preparation for the SAT.

However, interestingly, equally large score gains were seen in 8% of people who did not receive any coaching. The researchers also found that 28–36% of people who received coaching either showed no change in their SAT scores or a deterioration in scores.

This study makes it clear that the effects of coaching are not the same for everyone and that, in some cases, coaching may even have a detrimental effect on performance. Remember, too, that studies such as this have no control over who receives coaching and who does not, and it's possible that at least some of the effects are due to people who are more likely to benefit from coaching opting for it.

An 11+ study
A study that is often quoted to support the benefits of coaching for the 11+ test was conducted in Northern Ireland. The authors of the study conclude that it 'clearly indicates the dramatic gain in test scores over a period of nine months'.

While the children in this study did show a large increase in their Verbal Reasoning scores, a number of unanswered questions about this study make interpretation less than clear-cut.

- Coaching was defined in a different way from that of many other studies. Although the children received a special three-hour coaching session during their nine months' preparation, most of what is referred to as 'coaching' was teachers providing 'any other form of material they would normally use to prepare students for the test' including 'effective test-taking strategies'. In other words, 'coaching' in this context was primarily the standard preparation children would normally receive in school.
- Coaching in this study took place over a nine-month period, but no details are given about how much time was given to preparation for the 11+ during this time. Children also participated in a variety of preparation activities over this period. This makes it impossible to conclude, with any certainty, whether any specific preparation activities would be more beneficial than others.

- The most notable gains in test scores were seen over the nine-month coaching period. During this time, however, children would also have been studying the curriculum and their cognitive abilities would still have been developing. Both of these factors will affect test performance, irrespective of coaching. As the study did not include any children who were not given coaching over this period, it's impossible to say how much of the observed increase in scores was due to coaching and how much to the normal educational process and maturation of the individual.

KEY MESSAGES FROM THE RESEARCH

- Preparation and coaching can have a beneficial effect on test performance, but this effect is much smaller than is often assumed.
- Intensive test preparation does not guarantee that test scores will increase. Some research has shown scores to remain unchanged or even deteriorate after coaching.
- The reasons for such variations are not understood, but may result from natural fluctuations in test performance over time rather than a negative effect from coaching.

However, you shouldn't let these findings detract from the positive effect of well-targeted preparation. Note that:

- research does support the importance of preparation for good test performance
- but, as a parent, you should have a realistic expectation of what test preparation can achieve – preparation will help children demonstrate their abilities through the tests, but is unlikely to affect their underlying ability in any significant way.

SO WHAT NEXT?

The next chapter brings together the research findings and GL Assessment's experience of test development to help you as a parent by:

- planning your own preparation and supporting your child in planning theirs
- targeting activities that are most likely to be beneficial
- using the time you and your child have to best effect.

WHAT CAN I DO TO HELP MY CHILD PREPARE?

- WHAT ARE THE BEST ACTIVITIES TO HELP MY CHILD PREPARE FOR THE 11+?
- WHAT OTHER SUPPORT CAN I GIVE MY CHILD?
- HOW MUCH TIME SHOULD WE SPEND ON PREPARATION?
- PREPARATION – FACT OR FICTION?

WHAT ARE THE BEST ACTIVITIES TO HELP MY CHILD PREPARE FOR THE 11+?

As we saw in Chapter 5, the available research provides an inadequate answer to this question. Nevertheless, based on what evidence is available, here are some ways you can use different types of preparation to improve your child's performance.

UNDERSTANDING THE QUESTION TYPES

This is one of the main areas targeted by intensive coaching. It aims to introduce each of the individual question types to test takers and to ensure that they understand the requirements of each. By working with your child to understand what each question type requires them to do and identifying specific strategies for each, you will be covering core 'coaching' activities. The *11+ Explained* series can be particularly helpful here.

TAKING PRACTICE TESTS

The 'practice effect' (that is, scores increasing when taking another test assessing the same abilities) is one of the most robust research findings. This emphasises the importance of using practice papers as part of effective test preparation.

Getting your child to take practice tests will be beneficial, as it gives them a better understanding of the test process and test instructions, plus familiarity with the layout of the questions, test paper and answer sheet. They will also learn how to approach timed tests. This should help to increase their confidence and reduce their anxiety about the 11+.

DEVELOPING TEST TECHNIQUE

Test technique encompasses many areas, but can be broken down into two categories:
- strategies concerning the test layout and how multiple-choice questions are presented
- strategies for managing performance during a strictly timed test like the 11+.

Being able to work quickly and accurately and not getting stuck on questions are all really important for achieving a good test score. So looking at the strategies above and knowledge of specific question types will help your child become familiar with the layout of the test paper and answer sheet and the nature of the questions, to ensure that they don't waste valuable time during the test.

DEALING WITH NERVES AND ANXIETY

Anxiety can be unpleasant and can potentially disrupt preparation by decreasing motivation. Anxiety is also known to have a negative effect on actual test performance.

Finding out about the test and the format of the questions it contains, along with practice at taking timed tests, will help your child feel more confident and consequently less anxious. Specific strategies for dealing with anxiety are also likely to be beneficial, to keep your child positive and focused and to prevent anxiety during the test itself interfering substantially with their performance.

We will explore both test strategy and dealing with nerves more fully in Part 2 of this *Parents' Guide*, so that you can help your child to give their best test performance possible.

WHAT OTHER SUPPORT CAN I GIVE MY CHILD?

You can be very effective in helping your child prepare for their 11+ without necessarily needing to draw extensively on external resources such as personal tutors or coaching programmes.

WORKING WITH YOUR CHILD

Much of this 'good preparation' can be covered by two simple activities:

- helping your child become familiar with the question types and the approach of the 11+ tests that they will be taking
- trying practice papers.

This *Parents' Guide* will help you:

- support your child in becoming familiar with what the tests require them to do, thus increasing their confidence and reducing anxiety, both of which benefit their performance
- understand about successful test technique and give you the knowledge you need to support your child in achieving their best performance
- support your child through the challenging experience of the 11+, helping them to understand and deal with the emotions they may experience.

THE OFFICIAL 11+ SERIES

GL Assessment's *Official 11+* preparation series will support you and your child throughout the 11+ process. It brings together GL Assessment's unique insight as provider of the majority of the real 11+ test papers plus the experience of the series authors in the 11+ and wider assessment, to cover core areas of effective test preparation. The resources will help you and your child become familiar with the demands of the 11+ tests, understand question strategies and develop test technique. In this way, the *Official 11+ Practice Papers* and the *11+ Explained* books, in conjunction with this *Parents' Guide*, provide the key activities and experiences needed for a comprehensive 11+ preparation course.

HOW MUCH TIME SHOULD WE SPEND ON PREPARATION?

There is no clear answer to this question, as the benefit a child gains from preparation depends on their individual starting point and needs. It also depends on the types of activities undertaken – for example, 10 hours spent on a range of activities is likely to be more beneficial than 10 hours spent practising a single question type.

What is clear is that most benefit is gained from the early stages of preparation because children tend to quickly grasp the essentials that will start to improve their performance, but more in-depth study (for example, of specific question strategies) will take more time. The benefit gained from five hours' work when first preparing for the 11+ will typically be greater than five hours spent after months of regular preparation.

As preparation therefore follows the 'law of diminishing returns', illustrated below, it's important for you to monitor your child's progress and encourage them to regularly move to new activities. This will help keep your child engaged with the preparation process and feel that they are making good progress.

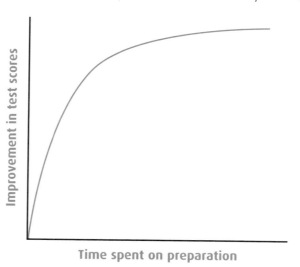

Time spent on preparation

WORKING WITH YOUR CHILD

Part 2 of this *Parents' Guide* provides advice on how to develop a structured preparation timetable with your child. This shows you all the essential elements that need to be incorporated into a timetable to enable your child to develop their skills, monitor their performance and recognise their successes.

Making the most of preparation time

- Make the best use of the time you have available for preparation and spread this time across a range of activities. Good preparation is about understanding and developing all the different skills that contribute to good test performance – your child using their knowledge of the individual question types, test strategy and good time management skills to let their ability shine through.
- Every child will need to spend a different amount of time on each type of activity to develop the necessary skills and become confident in their ability. Therefore, we can only provide initial guidance about what proportion of time you may want to spend on the different activities. The observations you make of your child as they progress with their preparation will be key to understanding when they need to move on to another activity. The *11+ Explained* books include Progress Charts, which will help you review progress with your child and know when it's time for them to move on to the next activity.
- The actual time spent on preparation may extend over a period of months or even up to a year. We don't recommend starting more than a year before the test – your child may become 'overloaded' if preparation spans too much time and will also find it difficult to stay motivated to work consistently towards an event that is too far in the future.
- Breaking preparation down into small, manageable chunks will be both more motivating for your child and also more beneficial for their learning and consolidation.

PREPARATION – FACT OR FICTION?

There is no doubt that good preparation for the 11+ is important for many reasons. However, we appreciate that preparation can be a source of concern for parents. This section dispels some of the 'myths' surrounding preparation.

- Preparation does help 11+ test performance, though the effects are modest and research shows that test improvements resulting from coaching are not as great as many commercial coaching providers might claim.
- Preparation is not about giving people 'an unfair advantage'. Instead, it's about helping individuals show their true ability by understanding the test, what's required of them and how best to approach it.
- There is nothing 'magical' about any sort of preparation – it involves familiarisation plus tips and techniques, coupled with motivated practice and learning. This helps children know how to show their true abilities.
- Preparation activities are not about making children 'smarter'. They are about letting their ability shine through the test rather than changing their ability.

As a parent, you can learn about all the essential elements of effective preparation and support your child through this journey. This *Parents' Guide* contains essential information that will develop your understanding of the 11+ test. You can draw on this information to support your child in their effective preparation for the 11+. Further information should also be available from your child's primary school and the school or Local Authority they are applying to.

- **HOW ARE THE 11+ SCORES CALCULATED?**
- **IS THERE A 'PASS MARK'?**
- **WHAT INFORMATION AM I LIKELY TO RECEIVE ABOUT MY CHILD'S 11+ RESULTS?**

HOW ARE THE 11+ SCORES CALCULATED?

The most basic type of score obtained from an 11+ test is called a 'raw score'. This is simply the number of correct answers.

In order to make the raw scores easier to interpret, they have to be 'standardised' using a special statistical process. This means that they are put onto a 'standard scale' and, in addition, the number of questions in the test and the child's age are taken into account. In this way, the 'standardisation' process removes the variable elements so that children can be compared equally.

How does standardisation help?

Standardisation allows the score from each test or combination of tests to be compared to those of other children who have taken the same test.

It also allows the scores from two or more tests to be added together meaningfully (for example, to produce a single score based on Verbal and Non-Verbal Reasoning tests) while taking account of different numbers of questions in each test and the difficulty of each test.

At this stage in their education, children's age is known to have an effect on their performance. This means that older children will, on average, perform slightly better in tests such as the 11+. The standardisation process allows the effect of children's age on test performance to be taken into account, meaning that a 'level playing field' is created for all age-appropriate children.

For these reasons, parents will usually just receive a standardised score rather than raw scores.

What is standardisation?

Essentially, standardisation involves taking the raw scores of every child who has taken the particular test and counting up how many have achieved each score, along with their age. This then allows any individual child's score to be interpreted relative to all the other children who took the same test.

For the 11+, standardisation can be carried out only after the test has been completed by all candidates, as exactly the same test will not have been taken before by those children. This process, referred to as 'local standardisation', is used for most 11+ exams. It differs from that used for many other educational tests, which are standardised on a general sample of children before the tests are used.

When test scores are standardised, the age of each child is also taken into account. Within any school year, age is known to have a modest effect on test scores – the older children in a year tend to perform slightly higher than younger children. Standardisation therefore uses both the raw scores obtained from the test and the age of each child. This ensures that standardised scores reflect a child's abilities and not their age at the time of taking the test.

What is the effect of local standardisation?

As local standardisation is conducted on the test results generated by all the children taking a test for one school or Local Authority in any given year, there are no external reference points such as national results or standards against which scores can be compared as there are with some forms of testing such as SATs and the *Cognitive Abilities Test*.

Instead, each child's results are reported relative to the group of children who took the test. While the tests themselves are designed to be of a comparable standard between years, a child's standardised score in the test will depend partly on the ability of other candidates who took the same test. For example, if in any one year there are a large number of very able children, then children will have to perform better than they might in a year where candidates were generally less able. 11+ scores cannot therefore be meaningfully compared to nationally standardised scores obtained from other tests that your child may take.

In only a very limited number of cases is the 11+ nationally standardised. National standardisation has no effect on the actual results that you will receive on your child's test performance or on how these results are used as part of the selection process. The only difference is that, as the 11+ has been standardised on a nationally representative sample, results reflect your child's performance relative to this wider group.

STANDARDISED SCORES

To summarise, the standardised score from an 11+ test represents how a child has done (in a single test or combination of tests) relative to other candidates who have taken the same test. As age is known to be related to ability, standardised scores include an allowance for age so that the test is fair to all children.

IS THERE A 'PASS MARK'?

Selective schools do not always necessarily have a set pass mark. However, some Local Authorities and schools will advertise the test score or combination of test scores that a child will need to achieve in order to qualify for a place. Each Local Authority or school sets their own admissions criteria, which will include how the test scores are used. However, there may not be an actual mark needed to qualify and, if there is, it will be different for each Local Authority or school. The reason for these differences is that the test scores may be averaged, combined or used individually, which means that the scale on which the decisions are made differs. Also, more or less able cohorts (or groups of children) may apply to different schools and therefore your child may need a higher score to qualify at one school where the group applying to the school is more able.

However, it is not necessarily the top-performing children that a selective school will offer their available places to. For example, some schools will offer places in their schools to children of a range of abilities, in order to achieve an intake representative of the group that originally applied. This local group may be more able or less able than a national average, but some schools consider it important to reflect the ability range of the local children.

Other schools may prefer to offer places to children representative of the ability range nationally. To achieve this, schools will not base their decisions on standardised scores, but on bands of standardised scores. There can be any number of bands, but generally 5, 7 or 9 bands are used. Once each child has been placed into a band, based on the standardised score they achieved, the school is then able to allocate places. Schools may offer places to:

- the top performing children in the top band
- children across the bands, representative of the range of abilities of the local applicants

- children across the bands, representative of national averages
- an equal number of children from each band.

It is therefore important that you research the specific requirements of each school you are applying to. Each school has to set out their admissions criteria, which are freely available to the public.

WHAT INFORMATION AM I LIKELY TO RECEIVE ABOUT MY CHILD'S 11+ RESULTS?

Although the exact information parents receive may vary between schools or Local Authorities, it is most common to receive the single score on which the selection decision is based. This will usually be a single score that indicates your child's performance in the 11+ test.

Where the 11+ test for a school or Local Authority comprised more than one test, the single score can reflect:

- the average of scores from all the tests taken
- the cumulative score from all the tests taken
- the best scores achieved from the tests taken (that is, where the child's weakest score in the tests they have taken has been dropped from the total, if they have taken more than one test in the same subject)
- where testing happens in two stages, the cumulative score achieved for both stages.

The exact way in which scores from multiple tests are treated is the decision of the school or Local Authority.

- **WHAT IS AN APPEAL?**
- **WILL THE APPEAL BE FAIR?**
- **WHAT WILL I NEED FOR AN APPEAL?**
- **WHAT HAPPENS ONCE I HAVE LODGED AN APPEAL?**

WHAT IS AN APPEAL?

You may feel that there are extenuating circumstances about your child, the circumstances surrounding the testing session or some other aspect relating to your child's life that you would like to be taken into account.

This is normally done through an appeal. The requirements and deadlines for lodging an appeal are usually detailed as part of the information you receive with the results and the school or Local Authority decision.

WILL THE APPEAL BE FAIR?

Each admissions authority must define their admissions policy and procedures in line with the School Admissions Code, to ensure that they are operating a fair, legal and ethical process for all.

Similarly, they must also define how they will deal with appeals against decisions. This policy and procedure must be in line with the School Admissions Appeals Code.

Copies of these codes can be obtained from the admissions authority to which you are applying.

WHAT WILL I NEED FOR AN APPEAL?

As part of lodging an appeal, you will usually be asked to supply some sort of evidence to verify the grounds on which you are appealing. This could be school results or reports, a doctor's certificate or letter, or other supporting documentation.

If your child is unwell on the day of the test, or there is a family bereavement or something occurs that you feel may have an adverse effect on your child, it's vital that you inform someone immediately. You should notify staff at the test centre by phone as soon as possible if you have decided not to attend the test session, or in person on arrival at the test centre, to explain the circumstances. It's also advisable to leave a letter at the test centre to confirm in writing the issues you are raising, or to do this as soon as possible.

Ensure that you have as much documentary evidence as possible from the test day and submit this as soon as possible afterwards (keeping a copy of everything).

Be as proactive as you can as early as possible, as it is not recommended to raise concerns once you have received the results. There are many legal teams who can support an appeal if you feel it necessary, but usually this is an unnecessary additional expense.

WHAT HAPPENS ONCE I HAVE LODGED AN APPEAL?

Once you have submitted an appeal and any supporting evidence, your case will be brought before an appeals panel. Members are trained to hear, deliberate on and decide whether there are grounds for appeal and whether the 11+ decision was correct. Appeals panel members are independent of the school or Local Authority to which you are applying.

The appeals process will usually involve you attending an appeals session, which might last an hour or more, to put forward your concerns and evidence and to discuss the details further with the appeals panel.

Appeal hearings are normally held within about a month of an appeal being lodged. The outcome of the appeal will be confirmed to you in writing. If the appeals panel finds in favour of the parent, the decision is binding on the admissions authority.

The appeals process is there to ensure that extenuating circumstances can be discussed and, if appropriate, taken into account when deciding whether a child has a place at their chosen school or not. The appeals process is stressful for all the family so should only be considered where there are truly special circumstances and a genuine case. It's worth knowing that the majority of decisions are upheld by appeals panels; however, some decisions can be investigated further and reversed.

There is also a School Adjudicator who is appointed to resolve issues like this if they can't be sorted out at a local level.

WHERE TO FIND INFORMATION

For further information or for copies of the Department for Education School Admissions Code, School Admissions Appeals Code and the Schools Adjudicator's documents, visit *www.education.gov.uk/schools/adminandfinance/schooladmissions.*

Whatever the outcome of the 11+, whether you have decided to appeal against a decision or not, it is important that you and your child take a positive view. Remember that not all schools are suitable for all children; with support and encouragement your child has the potential to succeed in any school and may excel in a non-selective school that better meets their specific needs.

PART 2

Supporting your child through the 11+

- **WHAT CAN I DO TO HELP MY CHILD PREPARE FOR THE 11+?**
- **WHAT SHOULD MY ROLE BE?**
- **HOW CAN I HELP MY CHILD STRUCTURE THEIR 11+ PREPARATION?**
- **WHAT NEEDS TO BE INCLUDED IN THE PREPARATION TIMETABLE?**

WHAT CAN I DO TO HELP MY CHILD PREPARE FOR THE 11+?

As a parent, you can do many things to help your child prepare for the 11+. In fact, much of this *Parents' Guide* focuses on helping your child work towards their 11+ test, once you have made the decision to enter them for it.

In Part 1 we identified general preparation activities through which you can support your child, such as:

- understanding question formats
- developing test technique
- taking practice papers.

Here we'll show you how to help your child structure their time by using a timetable. This will bring together the general preparation activities that were identified in Part 1 of the *Parents' Guide* with the specific activities that are now covered in Part 2:

- using practice papers
- learning about question types
- developing speed and accuracy
- enhancing test technique
- doing additional practice activities
- final preparation.

To support your child effectively, you will also need to develop your own understanding of the 11+. This *Parents' Guide* will help you do this, as will GL Assessment's *11+ Explained* series, which presents the main question types for Verbal and Non-Verbal Reasoning. Our website (*www.officialelevenplus.co.uk*) and the information provided by your school or Local Authority will also be very valuable to you.

WHAT SHOULD MY ROLE BE?

As well as helping your child structure their preparation and supporting them when working on the sorts of activities listed above, you have an important role to play in several other areas.

HELPING YOUR CHILD UNDERSTAND THE ADMISSIONS PROCESS

Your child will be more motivated if they understand the admissions process generally and the role of the 11+ tests in this. So you should ensure that they understand what will happen and how their 11+ results will be used by the school(s) to which they are applying.

DEVELOPING AN UNDERSTANDING OF THE 11+ TESTS

Use your own understanding of the 11+ tests to help your child understand the specific requirements of the different tests that they will be taking. We recommend that you also try practice questions yourself and think about how you solve them, so you can help your child understand the best way of approaching different question types. The *11+ Explained* series will give you more specific tips on how to tackle each question type. You should also work with your child to review their performance on questions, to identify what skills they need to develop.

SUPPORTING YOUR CHILD IN SPECIFIC ACTIVITIES

Help your child with specific activities, such as taking practice tests under timed conditions to make the experience more authentic. Also, support them in games or other activities practising 11+ skills that require another person.

HELPING YOUR CHILD DEVELOP OPTIMUM TEST PERFORMANCE

Work with your child to understand and try out the tips and strategies necessary to achieve their best performance. Give your child feedback on how effectively they are applying these to 11+ questions and practice tests.

MANAGING EMOTIONS AND BUILDING CONFIDENCE

Help your child manage the challenges of the 11+ by using their positive emotions to encourage and build confidence and helping them to deal constructively with their more negative emotions.

PROVIDING MOTIVATION AND FOCUS

Provide ongoing encouragement and motivation throughout your child's preparation and in the build-up to the 11+ itself, keeping them focused and committed to doing their best in the test.

PROMOTING LEARNING AND DEVELOPMENT

In many ways, parents will work in the same way as a teacher would to support their child in acquiring the new knowledge, skills and understanding they will need to do their best in the 11+. Throughout your child's 11+ preparation, you should be aware of the type of support that your child needs to help promote their learning and development. Consider:

- what your child is currently doing (for example, their progress on a specific question type)
- what they need to be able to do (for example, the strategies they need to use to answer questions effectively)
- how you can help them make progress (for example, using your understanding of the question type to support their learning)
- knowing when your support is needed and is effective and when you can leave your child to practise their new skills independently (for example, by monitoring your child's use of the strategy and the effect this has on their success in the question type).

Let's start by looking at how you can help your child structure their preparation.

HOW CAN I HELP MY CHILD STRUCTURE THEIR 11+ PREPARATION?

Your child will need to learn many new skills and carry out various activities as they work towards the 11+ test, so they will need to make the best use of the time available. This means that it's essential to develop a timetable with your child to structure their preparation.

You have an important role in guiding your child through what they should be doing and when, and prompting them to get on with it! You will also need to encourage and support your child emotionally throughout the build-up to the 11+ and afterwards (see Chapters 11 and 14).

Tailoring a timetable for your child

Effective preparation for the 11+ needs to cover three elements, which then provide an overall framework for the timetable.

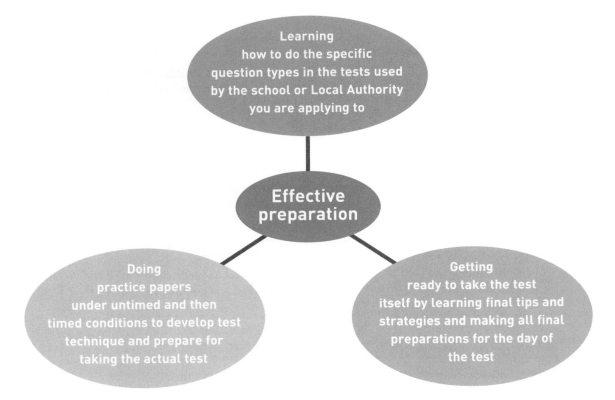

Each of these elements will need to be broken down into a number of specific activities. For example, learning about specific question types will involve understanding the question type, learning strategies to tackle it, trying practice questions and reviewing progress. These activities will usually be spread out over a period of time to allow time for learning, practice, reflection and consolidation.

Although every timetable needs to include these common elements, it can then be adjusted to your child's particular needs. For example, if you know your child is weaker in one area, then you would probably want to allocate more time to this. Tailoring your timetable is simply about being aware of your child's specific strengths and needs, plus other external factors such as existing commitments, to create a timetable that is realistic and likely to be most effective.

Involving your child

Developing the timetable with your child, and involving them from the beginning of their preparation, will bring a number of benefits.

- **Commitment:** As your child sees their ideas and contributions developing into a timetable, this will add substantially to their commitment to the process. It's also important to show your commitment both to the 11+ and helping your child work towards it.
- **Confidence:** Knowing that their contribution has been taken seriously and their ideas and concerns listened to will increase your child's confidence in being able to work successfully towards the 11+.
- **Understanding:** They will gain a clear understanding of what their 11+ preparation involves – what they need to do and when.
- **Achievement:** They will gain a sense of achievement both from working with you to develop the timetable and as they reach the success points within it.

Developing the timetable together will ensure that your child is motivated in their 11+ preparation. By involving them at this stage, they are much more likely to be committed to achieving the targets they have helped set – especially if some small rewards are given for achieving the goals! (See page 52 for more on targets.)

WHAT NEEDS TO BE INCLUDED IN THE PREPARATION TIMETABLE?

To answer this question, you must first find out all the relevant information that you need to start developing your timetable.

Information needed

Make sure that you have considered the following questions:

- When will the 11+ test take place and how long do you have for preparation?
- Which subjects are your school or Local Authority testing?
- What other materials are you going to use? We have referred to the support GL Assessment's *11+ Explained* books and *Official 11+ Practice Papers* might offer, but if you are looking for other resources, we recommend that they:
  - cover a good range of questions types (examples of all Verbal and Non-Verbal Reasoning question types that may appear in the 11+ tests are included in the Appendix to this book)
  - are from a reputable source – looking at what else is in the publisher's portfolio and reviews of these materials can be useful here
  - make realistic claims about the likely effect they will have on a child's chances of success
  - have been reviewed by independent sources or recommended by other parents or teachers.
- Is there sufficient time available in your child's existing weekly schedule to fit in 11+ preparation, or will they need to spend less time on their other activities?
- What other significant events are going on in your lives between now and the test itself (for instance existing commitments to learning, family events, other activities your child regularly participates in). What effect might these have on preparation, and how will you factor the time needed for these into your preparation timetable?

When to start preparation

Knowing how long you have before the test is an essential starting point in developing a timetable, as you need to work backwards from the time of the actual test. As you read this and begin your preparation, you may have a few months, a year or even more before your child takes their 11+ test.

It's not uncommon for parents to start considering options for secondary schools more than one year in advance. While we would not discourage starting 11+ preparation earlier, we would also strongly advocate that there is no need for your child to start preparing for the 11+ more than a year before the test. Given a well-structured approach and good motivation, a year gives plenty of time to cover all the essentials. Another reason not to start too early is that, if your 11+ test includes Maths and English tests, some of the content of the tests may not yet have been covered in the curriculum. This might cause your child to feel anxious if they come across questions with unfamiliar curriculum content at an early stage in their preparation.

The sample timetables given here assume differing amounts of time before the test – 12 months, 6 months and 3 months. They also largely follow the approach used in the GL Assessment *11+ Explained* books – starting with understanding the individual question types and then working on test-taking skills in the build-up to the test itself.

We recommend you choose the timetable that is closest to the time you have available before your child's 11+ test and use this as a starting point for helping your child develop a timetable of their own. The time allocated to activities in the sample timetables is notional, so please work out what will be most appropriate for your child, according to their individual needs.

TRANSFERRABLE SKILLS

Preparing for the 11+ can be a complex task and there are many things to consider when developing a timetable. Your child will need to think about the different activities they have to do and which they need to do first, then allocate different amounts of time to each. Children will be able to use these valuable planning and organisation skills in other situations both now and later in their lives.

Understanding the sample timetables

These notes will help you understand the sample timetables and the key differences between them, depending on the amount of time available for preparation.

- The same core elements – learning about the question types, developing test technique and final preparations – are included in each timetable, regardless of how long is available for preparation.
- All elements appear in approximately the same order in each timetable.
- More activities need to be carried out at the same time as each other in the build-up to the test itself. This is because, in the last few weeks before the test, your child will be bringing together all their learning and doing any final reviews and consolidation they need.
- The more time that is available for preparation, the more it is possible to space out the activities, particularly at the beginning.
- Where more than one activity is indicated as occurring at the same time, the timetables do not imply that the amount of preparation time needs to expand greatly. Some activities will require only short 'recaps' (for instance, a quick review of a question type to make sure that a particular strategy for solving it is being used correctly). Some will need to be done only occasionally (for example, taking a practice paper to review speed and accuracy).
- In timetables with shorter preparation times, some activities need to begin earlier in the sequence to allow for learning to occur over a period of time. For example, you will probably want to start reviewing progress on question types soon, to make sure that you have plenty of time for any additional study needed. You can see examples of this in the sample timetables later in this chapter.
- With all timetables, there needs to be a considerable degree of flexibility to adjust to the needs of your child as they progress towards the test.

The sample timetables include the following activities or stages of preparation:

- **Practice papers:** These are used mainly towards the end of preparation and should usually be taken under timed conditions. They will help your child develop test technique and prepare for the demands of taking the test itself. However, you may also want to give your child a practice paper at the beginning of their preparation, so they can see what all their preparation is building up to and to give you a 'benchmark' against which to track progress.
- **General 11+ familiarisation:** This is to make sure that your child understands everything they need to about the 11+ in a broad sense – what it is, its purpose and how it will be used by schools.
- **Question types:** Understanding the different question types is a significant part of preparation and will involve your child systematically working through the different question types they may encounter to ensure that they know what each question type requires them to do, how they can go about solving it effectively and then practising it.
- **Review all progress:** After they have spent some time learning about the different question types, your child should review their progress to see whether there are any question types that need further study.

- **Practise question types further:** Your child should go over any specific question types that they have identified as needing further work.
- **Develop speed and accuracy:** Here, your child will mainly be using practice papers to develop their ability to work both quickly and accurately under timed conditions, as described in Chapter 12.
- **Additional activities:** As your child becomes familiar with the question types, they can try additional activities designed to help them with various question types. GL Assessment's *11+ Explained* books include 'Verbal Fun' and 'Non-Verbal Fun' activities, which give your child the chance to build up their skills and consolidate learning more informally.
- **Final preparation:** In the few days before the test itself, there are various things you and your child will need to do to make sure that everything goes as smoothly as possible on the day of the test itself, as described in Chapter 13.
- **Success points:** These are indicated at various points on the timetables and show 'milestones' in your child's preparation for the 11+. More information on setting success points or goals is given in Chapter 10.

A NOTE ON 'SUCCESS POINTS'

In the sample timetables, the success points are given for illustrative purposes only. Success points should be tied to 'meaningful' achievements, such as learning about a specific question type or group of question types, so their exact timing will depend on the type of test and also your child's progress. As many success points will be tied to progress rather than time (that is, 'when this point has been reached' as opposed to 'in this week'), success should be recognised when specific milestones are achieved.

Sample timetables

12 months' preparation time before test

	Weeks																																			
	1	2	3	4–24*	25	26	27	28	29	30	31	32	33	34	35	36	37	38	39	40	41	42	43	44	45	46	47	48	49	50	51	52
Practice paper	▓									▓			▓			▓			▓				▓				▓				▓	
General 11+ familiarisation	░																														░	
Question types			▓	▓	▓	▓	▓	▓	▓	▓	▓	▓	▓	▓	▓																	
Review all progress							▓	▓	▓	▓	▓	▓	▓	▓	▓	▓	▓	▓	▓	▓	▓	▓										
Practise question types further																	░	░	░	░	░	░	░	░								
Develop speed and accuracy															▓	▓	▓	▓	▓	▓	▓	▓	▓	▓	▓	▓						
Additional activities								░		░		░	░		░	░						░		░	░	░	░	░	░			
Final preparation																															▓	▓
Success points				*				*				*			*				*			*		*	*	*			*		*	*

* During weeks 4–24, include 'success points' every 3–4 weeks.

6 months' preparation time before test

	Weeks																									
	1	2	3	4	5	6	7	8	9	10	11	12	13	14	15	16	17	18	19	20	21	22	23	24	25	26
Practice paper																										
General 11+ familiarisation																										
Question types																										
Review all progress																										
Practise question types further																										
Develop speed and accuracy																										
Additional activities																										
Final preparation																										
Success points				*			*			*			*		*		*		*			*			*	*

3 months' preparation time before test

		Weeks												
		1	2	3	4	5	6	7	8	9	10	11	12	13
Practice paper		■							■	■			■	■
General 11+ familiarisation		■											■	
Question types		■	■	■	■									
Review all progress						■	■	■	■	■	■			
Practise question types further							■	■	■	■	■	■	■	
Develop speed and accuracy								■	■	■	■	■	■	■
Additional activities									■	■	■	■	■	
Final preparation														■
Success points			*		*		*		*	*		*	*	*

Detailed breakdown of a 2-week period

To help you understand more about how a timetable may work in practice, this section from the 6 months' timetable shows a more detailed breakdown of what a child might be doing during a 2-week period.

	Week 1							Week 2						
	Mon	Tues	Weds	Thurs	Fri	Sat	Sun	Mon	Tues	Weds	Thurs	Fri	Sat	Sun
Overview of NVR question type and what it requires you to do	10 minutes													
Review strategies for answering this question type and try them out	20 minutes													
Practise NVR question type						15 minutes								
Score and review practice questions						5 minutes								
Have a go at an additional NVR activity								30 minutes						
Review progress on first three NVR question types and identify further work that needs to be done and put time for these in timetable											25 minutes			

- **HOW CAN I MOTIVATE MY CHILD?**
- **HOW CAN I HELP MY CHILD LEARN MORE EFFECTIVELY?**

HOW CAN I MOTIVATE MY CHILD?

Preparation will be challenging for both you and your child, but will also offer lots of opportunities for new learning, working together and a sense of achievement. Getting motivation right will be key to success.

As a parent, you will be very experienced in motivating your child, even if you don't realise it. This experience will be invaluable as your child needs to be motivated and committed in order to prepare effectively for the 11+ test.

In this chapter we'll help you think about practical ways to motivate your child. We'll also consider how you can help your child make sure that their learning is really effective and show you how this can be applied to 11+ preparation.

What motivates your child?

A useful way to start thinking about how you can motivate your child is to explore 'external' and 'internal' motivators.

EXTERNAL MOTIVATION

External motivators are often associated with 'rewards', such as being given a treat or being allowed to do something that we find enjoyable. Such external motivators are often linked with doing things that other people want us to do. For example, you may reward your child for helping out around the house. Your child may not necessarily enjoy doing household chores, but they do them because they value the reward that you give them in return.

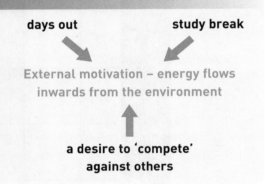

days out   study break

External motivation – energy flows inwards from the environment

a desire to 'compete' against others

INTERNAL MOTIVATION

By contrast, internal motivation comes from within the individual. It encourages us to do things because we enjoy and see the value in what we are doing, or are challenged by the idea of improving ourselves and seeing what we can achieve.

sense of mastery   learning new skills

Internal motivation – energy flows outwards from the individual

personal achievement

Developing motivation in your child

Both external and internal motivation will play an important part in 11+ success. Though it may seem simplest to motivate your child through external motivation, this is not the whole answer. External motivation can be difficult to sustain over extended periods because motivators can lose their value if they are used too often and can place an ever-increasing demand on those providing the external motivators. If children come to rely too heavily on external motivators to energise them for their 11+, this can also have the negative effect of reducing their internal motivation.

For these reasons, an ideal balance needs to consist of more motivation coming from within the child and less being external. An important part of this will be involving your child in the decision to take the 11+ and planning their preparation (see Chapter 9). You can also develop internal motivators in the following ways:

- Encourage your child to see the 11+ as a challenge and explain to them about all the new learning that will accompany their preparation activities.
- Make sure that your child celebrates their successes and that you recognise their efforts.
- Help your child to recognise the importance of what they are doing – get them to see the 'bigger picture' of the 11+ and the implications that this may have for their future education.
- Make connections between the skills they are learning for the 11+ and how these can be applied to other aspects of their education and life more broadly (for example, test technique can be applied to other tests; planning and organisation skills can be used in other contexts).

Motivation should be positive at all times. Your child should be rewarded for what they do, so that they work towards achieving a reward. They should never lose a reward or be stopped from doing something they enjoy, if they don't reach a target.

REWARD EFFORT TOO

It's important that your child's effort is rewarded at least as much as achievement. Many studies have shown that, if children are rewarded for their *effort*, they will persevere and deal better with setbacks than if they are rewarded for achievements such as how well they do in a practice test. Encourage your child to try their best, regardless of outcome, as it develops the motivation to keep trying. This motivation will become one of the foundations of success at the 11+. It will encourage your child to work hard to learn new skills and to develop their natural abilities and let these show through in the 11+ test.

The key ingredients of motivation

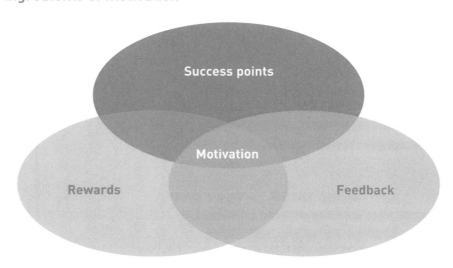

Identifying success points

These are the targets or goals that you need to agree with your child. They are an important aspect of the preparation plan we explored in Chapter 9. Your child needs to know exactly what they have to do in order to achieve them.

Success points may either be:

- time-related (for example, 'learn about two question types per week for three weeks'), or
- more flexible in terms of time as they are related to when a certain activity is complete rather than a set time (for example, 'review all question types and work through any that need to be revised further'). In this example, *what* needs to be achieved is clear but *when* this success point will be reached will depend on how many question types need to be reviewed and how quickly they are reviewed.

Success points don't need to be evenly spaced throughout preparation, but they should be fairly regular and the gaps between them shouldn't be too long or require too much work from your child. Their purpose is to keep your child motivated and looking forward, but this will be less effective if the next goal is too far ahead.

You should also consider key success points such as completing all the preparation for the 11+ and taking the 11+ itself. These will be big events for your child and you should celebrate them together. As with other success points, this will recognise the effort your child has put in and clearly show the value you place in this.

Remember, success points should mainly be related to effort rather than achievement. Rewarding effort is one of the surest ways of keeping your child engaged and focused on their preparation.

Getting rewards

These serve as an important way of recognising that your child has reached their success points. Rewards can take many different forms and can be thought of as providing 'external' or 'internal' motivation, as discussed earlier in this chapter.

Rewards don't have to be significant, material rewards. Rewards such as giving your child time to do what they enjoy or doing a fun activity with them can be great motivators, particularly if they have given up some activities to focus on the 11+. Doing things with your child or sharing a reward with the whole family is also a good way of helping your child feel fully supported and realise that everyone recognises their effort.

You will know what rewards will appeal most to your child and you should discuss and agree these with them when developing their preparation plan.

Giving feedback

Feedback is probably the most important element of learning and development. It shows us how we are doing in working towards our goals and can provide a corrective 'steer' if your child is not making best use of their preparation time.

Feedback may be embedded in the tasks that your child is doing – for example, checking the answers to practice questions they have attempted or scoring practice papers. This type of feedback is built into the *11+ Explained* books to give your child the opportunity to check their progress regularly.

You can also play a key role in giving your child feedback. Much of your feedback is likely to be informal, by providing your insights and comments on how your child is doing. Most parents instinctively provide regular feedback to their children, but it will be particularly important to do this for 11+ preparation, as the skills involved in mastering the Verbal and Non-Verbal Reasoning tests may be completely new to some children.

EXAMPLES OF TYPES OF FEEDBACK

- Recognising your child's progress and making sure that they can see how much work they have done.
- Getting them to see how they are doing on practice questions and what they need to do as a result of this.
- When they seem stuck or not to be working that productively, helping them to realise this and prompting them to find a different way of doing things or to change activity.

A lot of your feedback will result from your observations of your child as they progress through their preparation. But, at times, it will also be useful for you to have a detailed understanding of the 11+ to help you provide more specific feedback, following the strategies provided in this book and GL Assessment's *11+ Explained* books.

This feedback process should help guide your child through their preparation, ensuring that they are working effectively and not getting stuck.

HOW CAN I HELP MY CHILD LEARN MORE EFFECTIVELY?

When preparing for the 11+, children need to be effective learners alongside developing skills in the areas tested by the 11+. To help you support your child's learning, we'll look here at a model of the 'learning cycle', which is based on the work of David Kolb.

It has long been recognised that learning is most effective when children play an active role in their own education, rather than passively receiving knowledge. One model that illustrates the active learning process is the 'experiential learning model' below, which highlights the importance of using our experiences as a starting point for developing our learning.

This model describes four linked stages, but it's often easy to overlook or pay insufficient attention to one or more of these stages. You may have come across similar models of the learning process that use slightly different terms. Each of these stages is distinct, but there is overlap between them as subsequent stages build on and develop ideas from previous stages.

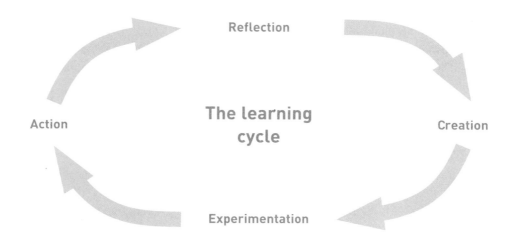

Reflection

Creation

Action

The learning cycle

Experimentation

How does the model help?

Each of the stages in the model can be applied to your child's learning during their 11+ preparation, as we will explain overleaf.

Action

It's possible to start at any point in the learning cycle, but the usual starting point for experiential learning is 'action'. Action is about doing something. In the context of the 11+, this may be trying out a new question type, completing an 11+ practice paper or trying out a new game or activity. Getting your child to do these activities will be the most important part of their 11+ preparation, but it's essential that they make the most of these opportunities and learn effectively from them. Using all the stages of the learning cycle model will make their learning most effective.

Reflection

Reflection then encourages us to stop and think about the actions that we have been doing. For example, if your child has just learned how to approach a new question type and tried a few practice questions, they then need to take time to reflect. This helps them consolidate their learning and review how effective it has been. They could ask themselves the following questions:

- What have I just learned?
- What went well?
- What did I find most difficult?
- How confident do I feel that I will be able to do what I have just done another time?

Your child's reflection needs to focus on what they have just done (for example, the practice questions or paper they have just attempted, or the test strategy they have just tried). You may need to help them do this by using questions such as those given above. Your child's initial responses may be quite general ('I found this question type hard'). However, for reflection to be most useful, encourage your child to think a bit more deeply by prompting them to be as specific as possible (Q: 'What was it about this question type that made it hard?', A: 'Finding the rule that links all the shapes together.').

Creation

Where reflection identifies issues, needs or things that could be done differently ('I don't think I used the strategy for tackling this question type very well'), creation should be used to generate ideas about how these issues can be addressed.

Try using the following questions to help your child think about how to create solutions to their issues:

- How could you do this differently next time?
- Is there anything else you need to be able to do or understand that would help?
- If you are finding a particular question type difficult, how else could you try to tackle it?

Creation is all about coming up with new ideas that will help your child's learning and actions to be more effective. But new ideas also need to be 'reality tested'. You can help your child do this by prompting them to consider how practical their ideas are and whether they are really likely to be helpful. The ideas that they come up with should help tackle the issues identified in the reflection stage. For example, learning to use the clock more effectively if they are running out of time on practice papers.

Experimentation

Experimentation is about trying out the new ideas your child has come up with during the creation stage, to see how they work in practice. These ideas may mean that your child tries small changes to refine what they are already doing well or tries completely new ways of approaching something in the 11+ that they have previously been struggling with.

Children will probably need some support during the experimentation stage. Encourage your child to try out fully the ideas identified during the creation stage. Working in new ways will require effort and motivation as it's often easier to keep doing things the same way. It helps if they realise they will need to try out a number of new ideas before they find the one that works best for them – you won't always get it right first time!

Using the model

Experiential learning goes beyond more 'academic' approaches to learning by reminding us to use our experiences and take time to review our learning. It's all too easy to move from one activity to the next without taking time to fully understand the benefits of the experience. When used well, experiential learning provides a highly effective method for children to learn the skills they need for the 11+, and elements of it are included in many approaches grounded in the psychology of learning.

Use the model to support how you work with your child, as a tool to help them develop their skills and performance. It will also stop them getting stuck by simply repeating the same actions again and again (for example, not using the best strategy to answer a particular question type they find difficult).

The experiential learning model should prove to be an effective way of working for your child. You can support your child by questioning them about activities they have just tried and exploring their responses during the reflection and creation stages of the learning cycle. Finally, you should encourage them to try new ways of approaching tasks during experimentation.

As your child becomes more familiar with the experiential learning model, they will start to learn more effectively. At first, you will need to encourage and support your child in the use of the learning cycle, but they will soon become more independent in using this to good effect in their 11+ preparation and, with practice, will quickly find themselves moving through the stages.

TRANSFERRABLE SKILLS

The learning cycle model can be used to ensure that learning from any experience is effective. Your child will therefore be learning a very valuable skill for all learning situations. At first you may need to encourage your child to go through the different stages of the model to make the most of their learning. Prompt them to take some time after a new experience to review what happened, consider how they could do it more effectively and then try out some of their ideas when they next get a chance.

- WHY ARE EMOTIONS SO IMPORTANT?
- HOW CAN I PUT THE 11+ INTO PERSPECTIVE?
- HOW CAN I MAKE THE 11+ A POSITIVE EXPERIENCE?
- HOW CAN I HELP MY CHILD WORK THROUGH THEIR EMOTIONS?
- ANY TIPS FOR STAYING POSITIVE?

WHY ARE EMOTIONS SO IMPORTANT?

This chapter looks at how you can make 11+ preparation and the test itself as positive an experience as possible, by understanding and working with the emotions that both parents and children will feel as they go through the process. All of the advice given here about understanding and managing how you feel applies equally to parents and children.

Any event that is a challenge like the 11+ will arouse a range of emotions – in your child and possibly in other members of the family too. Some of these emotions may be positive, others negative, but all should be recognised as a natural and valid reaction to the situation. There are no 'right' or 'wrong' ways to feel, because the different reactions people have to similar events are an essential part of our individuality.

The emotions you and your child experience indicate how important the 11+ is to you. While you may sometimes wish that the 11+ were a less emotional issue, emotions play an essential role in your child's preparation.

POSITIVE EMOTIONS ...

- ... encourage your child to prepare by signalling the importance of the 11+
- ... motivate your child to keep working hard because, if they feel good about what they have achieved, they will recognise the progress they are making
- ... energise and stimulate your child, both during the good times and when things are tough
- ... reassure your child by reinforcing their successes and showing them that they are indeed capable of doing well, which builds the confidence necessary to perform well in the 11+.

Feelings of anxiety and apprehension about the 11+ are also completely normal and can be a good thing. Some anxiety will signal the importance of the 11+ to you and your child, and will help to focus their attention on preparation and doing their best. Too much anxiety, however, has the opposite effect as it will interfere with preparation by making it difficult for your child to keep focused and to learn. During the test itself, high levels of anxiety are known to have a negative effect on test performance as they can distract and make it more difficult to concentrate.

One way we can help manage the emotions aroused by the 11+ is to take a realistic and objective view of them – recognising the importance of the 11+ but not letting it impact on all aspects of your child's life.

11+ EXPLAINED

GL Assessment's *11+ Explained* books include advice for your child on how they can stay positive and deal effectively with their emotions. Here we'll cover similar areas, but in greater depth and more from the perspective of you, the parent. While children can readily take on some simple tips for managing their emotions, this will be far more effective if accompanied by parental support, in an environment that is accepting and nurturing towards everyone's feelings.

HOW CAN I PUT THE 11+ INTO PERSPECTIVE?

For anyone who has made the decision to work towards the 11+, or indeed any challenge, it will inevitably be an important part of their lives during this time.

However, it is essential you put the 11+ into perspective to ensure that it does not dominate the lives of you and your child, and possibly the rest of your family. You all have to get on with your daily lives and the 11+ will only be one part of this.

Putting the 11+ into perspective will also reduce its potential negative emotional impact, so that your child does not feel under undue pressure. If they feel anxious, this will affect their overall happiness and severely hamper their ability to prepare for the 11+ effectively. You may also want to be careful about what you take on board from other parents; just because they may be very anxious about the 11+, it does not mean that you should be also.

Practical ways to put the 11+ in perspective

- The 11+ is only one of the many things that will be going on in your family's life. Keep it in perspective and try not to let it affect your family more than it should. Be particularly alert to the process affecting other members of the family who are not directly involved in it, as this may cause resentment and create an unwelcome source of tension.
- Your child may have to put off or spend less time doing some things they enjoy, such as hobbies or seeing friends regularly, to allow enough time for their 11+ preparation. However, it's very important that their hard work is balanced with some fun and relaxation.
- Preparing for the 11+ is a big commitment, but it will soon be over. Keep your child focused on the date of the test and on their preparation timetable, but also help them see beyond the 11+. If they have stopped doing some activities they enjoy when preparing for the 11+, remind them that they will soon be able to start doing these again.
- During the 11+ preparation, it's always good for your child to have something to look forward to in the near future. Spending time with family and friends or doing things they enjoy will take your child's mind off the 11+ and so help them keep it in perspective.
- As the 11+ is a selection test designed to differentiate between able children, it's quite likely that your child will struggle with question types or practice papers at times. When this happens it's vital to recognise that, although the abilities assessed by the 11+ are important, they are only one part of your child's wide range of abilities. Remind your child that there are many things that the 11+ does not measure that they are good at. Don't let difficulties with particular tests spill over into negative views of their abilities more generally ('I can't understand this Non-Verbal Reasoning question, so I'll never pass the 11+').
- There will always be children who are more or less able in certain areas than your child, and competition with others will inevitably bring disappointment at some point. All you can expect of your child is that they do their best and keep focused when preparing, so that they do themselves justice in the test.
- Success is a great way of emphasising positive aspects of a challenge like the 11+. It also helps to minimise more challenging parts by ensuring that plenty of attention is given to successes and what is going well, rather than those parts of the 11+ that are found more challenging. This is why it's important to recognise your child's successes throughout their preparation and afterwards.
- During preparation, your child will be developing many skills that will help them in other areas of school and beyond. By highlighting this, you will help them understand the wider relevance of many of their preparation activities.

HOW CAN I MAKE THE 11+ A POSITIVE EXPERIENCE?

Dealing with the emotions that surround the 11+ can be difficult. Parents won't only be faced with the emotions their child is feeling, but are likely to experience many emotions themselves. Addressing these emotions, however difficult, will help you both maintain the positive outlook that is key to helping your child prepare.

To help you and your family deal with all these emotions, you should encourage an environment in which:

- everyone feels they can openly express the emotions they are feeling, when they are feeling them
- all emotions are recognised as being valid and there are no 'right' or 'wrong' ways of feeling
- family members are supported in understanding and working through their emotions, so that these help rather than hinder 11+ preparation.

Manage your own emotions

One of the most important starting points in helping your child deal with their emotions is to accept, understand and manage how *you* are feeling. If your concerns about the 11+ spill over into anxiety, frustration or even anger, this will have a particularly negative effect on your child. If you know the 11+ is a significant source of concern for you and is affecting your emotions, use the ideas in this chapter to help you try to feel more positive. Whatever you are feeling, always be careful how you express strong emotions around your child.

At times, emotions felt by parents and children may be very similar but, just as often, parents and children are likely to experience quite different emotions. Differences in how you and your child feel about the 11+ can be a significant source of tension and conflict. Sometimes tensions may arise without us knowing exactly why. This can often be because we are not fully aware of our own emotions, even though they have a strong influence on what we say and how we behave. It's therefore important to pay attention to how we are feeling and not to dismiss our emotions about the 11+.

Recognise your child's successes

Positive emotions will most often be linked to an achievement or success of some kind and this is why it's essential to recognise your child's successes.

Your child's preparation plan provides a structure to the activities they need to complete in the build-up to the 11+ and should include 'success points' or goals (see Chapter 9 for how to build these into a timetable for preparation). You should make sure that your child uses their plan to regularly monitor their progress and recognise their achievements. Celebrate when they reach their success points, as this will provide a great source of positive emotions for your child. Make sure that they take time to enjoy and take pride in what they've achieved rather than immediately moving on to the next task. This will help your child sustain their motivation throughout the preparation.

MAKING THE 11+ EXPERIENCE POSITIVE: KEY POINTS

- Develop an environment at home that is supportive to expressing, recognising and understanding emotions.
- Encourage your child to pay attention to their feelings. This will make it less likely that emotions will get in the way of effective 11+ preparation, so helping them remain positive and generally happy.
- Encourage your child to express their feelings and let them know that all emotions are equally valid.
- Be aware of your own emotions and make sure that they don't adversely affect how you interact with your child.

HOW CAN I HELP MY CHILD WORK THROUGH THEIR EMOTIONS?

Working constructively with our emotions is a skill that can be developed. All children learn the essential elements of this as part of their natural development. This includes the ability to identify different emotions, understand why they are feeling like this and deal with their feelings constructively.

When working with a new challenge like the 11+, your child's emotions will be valuable indicators of their successes (for example, when they are feeling proud of their achievements) and difficulties (for example, when they are struggling to understand a question type).

Your support and experience will help your child deal with their emotions that are linked to the 11+ in a positive way. So, how can you help them do this? The first vital step is for you to be aware of *how* your child is feeling, so you can then help them understand and work through these feelings.

Understanding your child's feelings

The following tips will help you work with your child to understand and use these emotions constructively.

- Your child's behaviour will often be a good indicator of how they are feeling about the 11+. So be aware of changes in their behaviour and take time to talk this through with them.
- Find out the causes of emotions. When your child shows strong emotions about the 11+, sometimes the cause of this will be obvious (for example, getting a lower than expected score in a practice paper) but, at other times, it won't be so obvious. Talk to your child about what they are thinking, as this will have an immediate impact on their feelings.
- Take time to pay attention to emotions. Help your child work through their feelings using questions like these:
  - How do you feel?
  - What were you doing when you felt like this?
  - What were you thinking at the time?
- Do a 'reality check' on their thinking. Try to understand what your child is thinking – this may require you to gently ask questions to uncover their thoughts ('Tell me what you are thinking?', 'Why do you believe that?').
  - If their thought is realistic ('I'm really struggling with this question type'), work with them to identify what they can do to change the situation.
  - If their thought is not realistic ('I should be getting all the practice questions right'), help them identify more realistic thoughts ('You can't expect to get all questions right every time, so let's set a target for how many you want to get right next time').

Now look at the diagram overleaf to see how you can work through your child's feelings.

Working through your child's feelings

Help your child work through their emotions by trying the following steps:

> Start by asking how they are feeling ('How are you feeling, you seem a bit unhappy?'). If they find it difficult to say, try getting them to explore their feelings more gradually ('Are you feeling happy or a bit worried?').

⬇

> Follow this up by asking what they were doing that made them feel this way ('When did you start feeling like this?', possibly followed by 'What were you doing that made you feel like this?'). This will help your child identify the trigger for their emotions.

⬇

> Then try to get your child to recall what they were thinking at the time ('What were you thinking at this time?', 'Do you know what caused you to feel this way?'). This may be difficult at first, as it's not something children – or even most people – are used to doing. It's also difficult because we most often focus on what we are doing rather than the thoughts that go on beneath our behaviours.

⬇

> When your child gives examples of how they were thinking, help them check how realistic these thoughts are.
>
> - 'Realistic' thoughts will usually relate to specific concerns about the 11+. These can be used to identify areas for development ('What do you think you need to do to change what you're thinking?').
> - 'Unrealistic' thoughts are those that go beyond the specific situation or are 'magnified'. Often specific difficulties or issues are generalised or spread out to other areas ('I can't do this question type, so I'll fail the 11+'). To address these, gently challenge your child to examine the thought to see how realistic it is ('How do you think you can get better at this question type?' or 'If you still find one question type hard, how could you work on this or do better in other parts of the test to make up for it?'). Be supportive and remind them of things they have done that contradict their assumptions. In this way, unrealistic thoughts can be changed into practical ideas for development ('It's OK not to get every question right; just try your best to get most of them right').

Always be encouraging and sympathetic when going through this process. Your child will probably find this difficult, particularly at first, but encouraging them to be realistic in their thinking is a very valuable way of helping them stay positive. Remember, no matter how unrealistic your child's thinking may seem, it is very real to them and so needs to be accepted and examined gently and supportively.

ANY TIPS FOR STAYING POSITIVE?

There are lots of things that your child can do to help stay positive. As we have started to explore in this chapter, what we think and feel are often closely linked. Our behaviour – what we *do* – also relates to how we *think* and *feel*. This means that taking positive action in any one of these three areas – **thinking, feeling or doing** – will have a positive effect on the other two.

The tips below give ideas about how you can support your child through each of these three areas – **behaviour** (what we do), **thoughts** and **feelings** – during their 11+ preparation.

You can help by explaining these tips to your child and encouraging their use when necessary. As with anything new, 'practice makes perfect'. So the more your child uses these tips, the more effective your child will be at staying positive.

Do

- Manage your child's preparation, so that they don't spend too long at any one time working on the 11+. Think about their preparation, what else they have had to do that day and your knowledge of their concentration span. Encourage them to keep focused during their preparation time, but then reward them by allowing them to do something completely different.
- 11+ preparation will mostly be desk-based work, so your child will benefit from opportunities to do physical activities and exercise. Physical activity is also a great way to help your child feel good and take their mind off worries about the 11+. Making sure that they eat well and get lots of rest will also help.
- Encourage your child not to talk too much to other children about the 11+, as this may make them more nervous. As other children may be preparing in different ways to suit their own needs, this can make your child wonder if they are 'doing it right'.
- Be organised, as this will help throughout your child's preparation and will prevent your child wasting time. It's particularly important to be organised in the build-up to the test and immediately before the test, so that children can see that they have done all the preparation they need to and know they are ready.

Think

- Encourage your child to think positively about their abilities, so they can rise to the challenge of the 11+ and enjoy the opportunities it offers to develop new skills.
- Encourage your child to think that it's all about doing the very best they can. The challenge should be to see how much they can improve and how well they can do, rather than how they do compared to their peers. While some element of peer competition is inevitable, and the 11+ is a competitive test, it's far more motivating and satisfying to set your own achievable yet challenging internal targets rather than always competing with others.
- Use the techniques described in this chapter to ensure that your child's thinking is 'realistic', so that specific difficulties in the 11+ won't affect their confidence more generally. Help your child to look at these difficulties as a way of identifying what they need to do to improve their performance, rather than letting problems damage their confidence.
- Work with your child to support their learning; remind them how much they have achieved and help them understand new concepts. This will build their confidence and give them a 'can do' attitude towards the 11+.

Feel

- If you see that your child is under stress, work with them to understand how they are feeling and why. Help them to have more positive thoughts than negative ones, for example by getting them to think about their successes.
- Be aware of your own feelings and don't let these spill over to your child, as they will be very receptive to your emotions and this can affect their behaviour.
- Allow your child some time each day to relax and do things they find enjoyable. This will help keep them positive and also 'recharge their batteries' for the preparation they still have to do.
- No matter what expectations you may have of your child, always show them how proud you are of them and what they are achieving. Encourage them to be proud, too. If they feel they have 'failed' or let you down, it may damage their confidence and de-motivate them. Remember, it's all about effort and trying their best – achievement will follow from this.

WHY IS TEST TECHNIQUE SO IMPORTANT?

All your child's preparation leads up to the test itself, where they will have a fairly short time to demonstrate their ability. Here we'll explore how you can help your child make the most of the time available in the test and thereby increase their chances of achieving a good score.

Ability alone won't guarantee a good score in the 11+. Your child needs to develop three further skills:

- understanding the format of the tests and the test questions
- knowing how to tackle multiple-choice questions
- knowing how to work effectively under timed test conditions.

As we saw in Chapters 5 and 6, preparation activities (particularly understanding different question types and taking practice papers) work on these areas to enhance children's performance. This chapter targets these three skills as they will help your child perform to the best of their ability in the actual test.

Think about how an athlete prepares for a race or a musician for a concert. They will have done years of training to develop their skills, but they still need further practice before each event to polish their technique and let their skills show through. Similarly, after preparing thoroughly for the 11+, your child will need to hone their test technique. This will make it easier for your child to 'get their knowledge out' during the test, help them make good use of the time available and know what to do if they get stuck.

HOW CAN PRACTICE PAPERS HELP?

Practice tests are an invaluable way of preparing for any test. If your child does only one thing to prepare for their 11+, we would recommend that they take a practice paper. Practice papers help your child with many of the core aspects of test preparation, including:

- familiarisation with the test instructions
- understanding question types and how they are answered. Often questions are multiple-choice, but standard-format questions are also used in some cases, where the child is required to supply their answers independently
- seeing the layout of the question booklet and answer sheet, and how these need to be used together
- familiarisation with the requirements of different question types
- gaining experience in switching rapidly between different types of question in a test.

If timed, practice papers will also get your child used to working quickly and accurately under timed conditions.

Developing an understanding of what to expect in the test itself will also increase your child's confidence and reduce potential anxiety.

A NOTE ON THE GL ASSESSMENT *PRACTICE PAPERS*

These offer your child the most authentic opportunities to prepare for the 11+, as they have ~~ developed by the same company that sets the majority of the actual 11+ tests. We recommend that you use these throughout your child's preparation for the 11+, though they will be particularly valuable in the final stages of preparation. Two packs of practice papers are available each for English, Maths, Non-Verbal Reasoning and Verbal Reasoning.

How do scores in practice tests relate to performance in the actual test?

Practice papers are generally designed to be slightly easier than the actual 11+ tests. This is because their purpose is to familiarise children with the test format and question types, and to give them opportunities to practise full tests under timed, but supportive, conditions.

Practice paper scores are:

● helpful in 'diagnosing' performance and identifying areas where more work is needed
● good for providing valuable feedback and motivation to your child.

However, owing to differences in question difficulty and the actual 11+ being scored differently, practice paper scores should be regarded only as very broad indicators of likely performance in the actual 11+ test.

WHY ARE ACCURACY AND SPEED SO IMPORTANT?

When working under timed conditions, two essential elements of good test performance are accuracy and speed.

The 11+ is a speeded test, which means that it's designed so that not everyone will complete all of the questions in the time allowed. Therefore, being able to work through the test questions accurately, yet rapidly, is a crucial skill for your child to master.

Here we use the terms 'accuracy' and 'speed' in the following way:

ACCURACY

This is the proportion of questions that your child tries and answers correctly.

SPEED

This refers to the number of questions in the test that your child attempts in the time available. Note that it doesn't take into account whether these questions are answered correctly or incorrectly.

To achieve their best possible score, your child needs to work both as quickly and as accurately as they can. Accuracy and speed will vary between children but, in the test, your child should:

● attempt as many questions as possible, if not all, in the time available
● answer correctly as many of these as possible.

TRANSFERRABLE SKILLS

Most tests that your child will take at school will be timed. Often the time limit means that it's necessary to work quickly and accurately in order to do well. The skills that your child is developing for the 11+ will therefore be very useful to them in the future.

HOW CAN I CHECK MY CHILD'S ACCURACY AND SPEED?

The best way of developing the skills of both accuracy and speed is to do 11+ practice papers. Practice paper scores indicate how well your child has performed, but can also be used 'diagnostically' to provide information on accuracy and speed of working. You and your child can then use this information to work out how they can develop their test technique.

> You can work out your child's accuracy and speed as shown below. If you prefer to simply look at general ways of improving their accuracy and speed, go to the blue section opposite and work through the tips with your child.

Working out your child's accuracy and speed

1   Give your child an 11+ practice test under timed conditions – try to replicate a timed test session as closely as possible.
2   When your child has completed the test, help them to work out their speed and accuracy scores:
    - *Speed of working:* Count how many questions your child has answered, irrespective of whether they are right or wrong. Divide this by the total number of questions in the test. For example, if there are 60 questions in the test and they attempted 45, then their speed is 45/60 = 0.75.
    - *Accuracy:* Count how many questions your child has answered correctly. Divide this by the total number of questions they have attempted (found above). For example, if they have correctly answered 32 of the 45 questions they attempted, then their accuracy is 32/45 = 0.71.
3   These scores will help you understand your child's approach to the test and how you can develop their test technique. Look at the table below for a more detailed description of your child's speed and accuracy.
4   If your child is taking 11+ tests in more than one subject (for example, Verbal Reasoning and Non-Verbal Reasoning tests), you should calculate your child's speed and accuracy separately for each subject, using appropriate practice papers. Their test technique in different subjects may vary considerably owing to factors such as level of ability and confidence in these. Children will therefore need to focus their development for each test type according to their needs.

What do the accuracy and speed scores mean?

There is no firm target for speed and accuracy scores for your child to aim at, as average speed and accuracy vary between different 11+ tests. However, the goal should always be for your child to work as accurately and as quickly as possible. Perfect speed and accuracy will mean that both scores calculated above are 1.

We wouldn't expect your child to be working both quickly and accurately when they first start taking practice tests. Since 11+ style tests are likely to be new to your child, it will take them time to get used to both the style of questions and how to approach the test more generally.

This table provides a general guide for interpreting how your child performed in a practice test, if you have calculated scores for accuracy and speed.

		Accuracy	
		Lower (0.00 to 0.80)	**Higher (0.81 to 1.00)**
Speed	**Faster (0.81 to 1.00)**	Your child answered a good number of questions, but many of those they attempted were answered incorrectly.	Your child answered a good number of questions and also had a good level of accuracy. Therefore, they tried most of the test questions, and many of those they attempted were correct.
	Slower (0.00 to 0.80)	Your child answered fewer questions and many of those they attempted were answered incorrectly.	Your child answered fewer questions, but had a good level of accuracy. Therefore they did not try that many of the test questions, but many of those they attempted were correct.

HOW CAN I HELP MY CHILD IMPROVE THEIR ACCURACY AND SPEED?

As we've explained, good test technique involves a balance between accuracy and speed. Your child should be pushing themselves to work as fast as they can – but not so fast that they make careless mistakes and get questions wrong that they are capable of answering correctly.

Use these tips for developing test technique

Accuracy and speed can always be improved, and the tips below show you how to do this.

 If you have worked out your child's accuracy and speed scores, go to the relevant section of these tips.

 If you haven't calculated your child's scores, go to the blue section below, which looks at the basics of developing accuracy and speed.

Lower accuracy, lower speed

If your child's scores fall into this category, they need to develop both their accuracy and speed.

Improving accuracy

Your child should start by looking at their accuracy, as before pushing themselves to work faster they should be getting a good proportion of questions they attempt correct.

- Review with your child how they have done on individual question types. There may be specific question types that they don't understand and so very poor scores on these may lead to a low accuracy score. If so, work through the specific questions types with your child, making sure that they understand what they need to do. The *11+ Explained* books will be particularly helpful here.
- If your child has not done particularly badly on any specific question types, it's still worth checking quickly whether there are any question types they find particularly challenging. If so, first work on these, as described above.
- If no particular question types are causing the issues, encourage your child to work quite slowly, one question at a time. Getting them to talk through how they approach the question and reach their answer can help you check whether they are making any basic errors and gives you an opportunity to correct them, if necessary. Also, when they are answering test questions, remind them to double-check all their answers to make sure that they have not made any unnecessary mistakes and are recording their answers properly on the answer sheet.
- Encourage your child to focus on one question at a time. If they find working under timed conditions too distracting or stressful, despite having a good understanding of the question types, they may need to try a practice paper under untimed conditions to build their confidence.
- When your child's accuracy has improved, they will then need to work on their speed.

$\longrightarrow$

Increasing speed

Speed is necessary for good performance in timed tests, but your child needs to make sure that their accuracy does not decrease as they push themselves to work faster.

- It can be challenging to keep focused consistently throughout a test but, if your child is distracted or their attention wanders, it's likely to have an impact on how many questions they attempt – and therefore their speed. While you can encourage your child to keep focused, this is difficult to teach directly. One effective strategy is to encourage your child to take short breaks during the test – putting their pen down and breathing deeply for 10 seconds between question types.
- Make sure that your child doesn't spend too long checking their answers. They should always do a quick check to make sure that they haven't made any unnecessary mistakes, but excessive checking or re-working will reduce their speed considerably and so is unlikely to improve their score. If they are approaching each question carefully, they should have confidence in the answer they arrive at.
- Encourage your child to work a bit faster than they would normally. You will need to do this before they start a timed practice test, encouraging focus, quick checks and any other time-saving strategies. (Strategies for different question types are included in the *11+ Explained* books.) Working faster will become more natural, with practice.
- Help your child to manage the time available for the test effectively. At the start of the test, get your child to check quickly how many questions there are and how long they have. They can then use this as a guide to ensure that they are on target to attempt most, if not all, of the test. However, do emphasise that this should be a quick check as they shouldn't waste test time doing precise calculations. Get your child also to check how long they have left, perhaps three or four times during the test, and encourage them to adjust their speed of working as necessary.

Lower accuracy, higher speed

If your child's scores are in this category, they need to slow down, so that they can improve their accuracy before building up their speed again.

Improving accuracy
- Your child first needs to slow down, so that they focus less on getting through so many questions and more on making sure that they get a higher proportion of the questions they do attempt correct. Reassure them that, at this stage, it doesn't matter if they don't answer all the questions as they can develop their speed once their accuracy has increased.
- Use the tips on improving accuracy given in the **blue box** on page 65.

Increasing speed
- When your child's accuracy has improved, use the tips given in the **blue box** above to help your child increase their speed again.

Higher accuracy, lower speed

If your child's scores are in this category, they need to increase their speed while maintaining their accuracy.

Increasing speed
- Use the tips given in the **blue box** above.

Higher accuracy, higher speed

If your child's scores are in this category, then both their accuracy and speed are good. However, there is always scope for improving their test technique further and practising it, so that it comes naturally when completing 11+ tests.

- To achieve top scores in the 11+ test, your child will need to work quickly and accurately throughout the test. They should use practice papers as an opportunity to practise keeping focused and ignoring any distractions, as well achieving good scores – they can relax as soon as the test is finished!
- Ensure that your child continues regular practice under timed test conditions and reviews their performance. Use these reviews to identify any further work needed on specific question types or test strategy. Resources such as the *11+ Explained* books also provide activities to further develop or practise specific question skills.

Monitoring your child's progress

To see how your child is progressing in developing their test technique, it's useful for them to take practice tests periodically. Practice tests will also help your child review their progress in different question types.

Whenever your child takes a practice paper, help them calculate their accuracy and speed to see how they are progressing. This, in turn, will help you and your child focus on what development activities will be most valuable for them next.

Your child is likely to benefit from taking practice tests more often as they get towards the end of their 11+ preparation and are developing their test technique. This may mean that they take practice tests once every couple of weeks in the two or three months before the 11+ test, with this becoming weekly in the last few weeks. However, be careful not to overwhelm your child with practice tests just before the 11+, as this may cause anxiety.

- **HOW CAN I HELP MY CHILD IMMEDIATELY BEFORE THE TEST?**
- **WHAT HAPPENS ON THE DAY OF THE TEST?**

HOW CAN I HELP MY CHILD IMMEDIATELY BEFORE THE TEST?

The final days before the test itself are a crucial time for your child. By this time they will have done most of the preparation they can. It's now important to support them through the final build-up – right up to when they enter the test centre.

For most children – and also many parents – concerns about the test may increase as the date draws closer. This is to be expected. For support on this, refer back to the advice on putting the 11+ into perspective and managing emotions given in Chapter 11.

Though it may be tempting to think that doing further preparation in the day or two before the test could make all the difference to your child, we would strongly advise against this. If your child has spent a number of months preparing, following a comprehensive and structured preparation plan, they will have done all the work they can for the 11+ test. Now's the time to check that you've made all the necessary practical arrangements and then do something to take your child's mind off the test.

Use the checklists below to make sure that you're fully prepared.

On the day before the test

- Discourage your child from doing any last-minute preparation. If they want to go over specific areas they feel nervous or unclear about, that's fine, but don't let them spend hours working away at practice papers or similar activities. It's unlikely to help their test performance and may cause your child to become tired or unduly anxious about the 11+, all of which could be detrimental to their performance on the day.
- Make sure that your child does something they enjoy – perhaps do something fun together. This will take their mind off the test and help them to relax.
- Check that you've made any necessary arrangements, such as travel, particularly if the test centre is not at your child's school.
- Be positive and reassuring, no matter how your child is feeling at this time. Remember also not to let your own concerns affect your child or influence how you behave with them.
- Make sure that you have checked through the information you have received from the school, to ensure that you understand the specific timings for the testing session at the school.
- Make sure that your child collects together everything that they will need for the test, particularly things like glasses if they wear them, or any medication they regularly take, plus any stationery needed and a drink, if they want one and this is allowed. Put these things somewhere obvious, so that you'll both remember to take them the next day!
- Make sure that your child doesn't go to bed too late – a good night's sleep before the test will help them feel fresh and alert. If you think your child might find it difficult to get to sleep owing to concerns about the test, try doing something active but mentally relaxing beforehand.

WHAT HAPPENS ON THE DAY OF THE TEST?

This is the big day for your child, so do everything you can to make them feel positive about themselves and their ability to do well. Also make sure that they are not distracted by other people or things going on around them. Going into the test session in a positive frame of mind and seeing it as an opportunity for all their hard work to pay off will give them a great platform for performing well.

On the day of the test

- Encourage your child to get up a little earlier than usual, so that there's plenty of time to wake up and get ready.
- Give your child a good breakfast with lots of 'energy' foods (for example, muesli, wholegrain bread, cereal or porridge). Avoid 'heavy' foods that may make them feel tired, like a big cooked breakfast.
- Encourage your child to wear comfortable clothes as they don't want to be distracted by feeling uncomfortable during the test. It's also a good idea to wear a number of layers, so it's easier for them to adjust their temperature if necessary.
- Leave plenty of time to get to the test centre – you don't want to be rushing and worrying about getting there on time. Remember that the local area will be much busier than usual with 11+ candidates making their way there; public transport may also be crowded. It may be difficult to find parking spaces nearby, so arrive early.
- Try to arrive early enough so that your child can have a little walk and get some fresh air before going into the test centre.
- Some schools will ask parents to wait in a large hall until children are finished and not leave the premises at all. Some schools may ask parents to leave their children at the school gate or inside the test centre, then return to collect them once the session is finished. The school will contact you, should your child become unwell, for example.

During the test

You may wish you could be in there with your child, but it's up to them to do their best when they enter the test room. However, the next best thing you can do is to go through the tips below together a few days before the test, as they will be helpful to your child during the test itself.

- Some friendly older children from the school your child is applying to may help out at the test centre. These children will have sat the tests themselves and will know exactly how children are likely to be feeling and how the day will go. Children should not be shy about approaching them if they have any questions.
- Advise your child not to talk much to other children taking the test before they all go in – if they're nervous, your child might become nervous too.
- Encourage your child to go to the toilet beforehand, even if they feel they don't need to – they don't want to be distracted during the test by feeling uncomfortable! Toilet breaks will be offered, but if children need to go to the toilet during the test session, they should put up their hand and quietly let the member of staff know what they need.
- Children may be instructed to take a seat in a large hall with all the other children, or may be split into smaller groups to take the tests in smaller rooms, possibly with children they already know from their existing school. They need to follow the instructions from the administrative staff.
- Children will be given breaks during the test session. They need to listen to instructions from the administrative staff.

$\longrightarrow$

- It is likely that children will be provided with everything they will need for the test.
- Tell your child that they should listen carefully to the instructions that are read out, no matter how many times they have taken practice tests. If they don't understand something in these instructions, reassure them that it's OK to ask.
- Point out that they should read all the written instructions carefully and re-read them, if needed, to fully understand what's required and to avoid making simple mistakes.
- Advise your child to keep calm and work steadily, remembering to check the time regularly. Make sure that they wear a watch, in case there's no clock in the room.
- Remind them to:
  - focus on one question at a time
  - use any strategies they have learned for each question type
  - eliminate any answer options they know are wrong and then make an informed guess for any questions they can't do
  - check all answers briefly
  - return to any questions at the end, if there's time.
- Stress that they should use all of the available time, right up until they are told to stop working, and not to give up before that.
- Suggest that your child avoids thinking about how other children are doing and to be positive about their own ability to do well.

HOW CAN I SUPPORT MY CHILD AFTER THE 11+ TEST?

After all the build-up to the 11+ test, make sure that you show your child how proud you are of them, as preparing for and completing the 11+ is a great achievement – whatever the final outcome.

Waiting for the results can be difficult for both parents and children. The relief of having completed the 11+ may soon be replaced by anxious anticipation of the outcome. As the day the results are released gets closer, it's natural to be concerned about the results and the effect they will have on you and your child's education. During this time of waiting, it's very important for you to continue to support your child – the 11+ selection process is not over until a final decision has been made on which school your child will go to.

The time immediately after the 11+ may be difficult for your child, as they wait for their results and no longer have the 11+ test itself to focus on. Make sure that this is a time of fun rather than anti-climax for your child, as a reward for all the hard work they put into their preparation. As it will be some time before the results are announced, it's good for them to keep busy to take their mind off worrying about the results. Make sure that they enjoy the extra time they now have, catching up with friends and activities that they may have had to put to one side during their test preparation.

The day will finally arrive when you will receive your communication from the school or Local Authority to which you have applied. This is normally done via letter or email, and will detail your child's results and whether your application for a place at your chosen school has been successful. In some areas, the results of the tests and the decision regarding the application may be communicated separately.

WHAT WILL TRANSITION TO SECONDARY SCHOOL INVOLVE?

Whatever the outcome of your child's 11+ test, they will shortly move to secondary school. Transition to any new school is recognised as being both an exciting and challenging time. Schools have become increasingly aware of issues around transition, looking at how to maintain children's motivation and attainment and avoid anxiety in their new environment. Therefore, schools actively work to support children through this process.

Recent research, commissioned by what is now the Department for Education, has identified a number of factors involved in successful transition from primary to secondary school. One of these is the adequate transfer of information. Schools should have established effective procedures for transferring information about children so that records of attainment and other academic information can be maintained. These procedures should happen automatically, although it may be worth checking that this is the case if you are moving between schools in different areas where links between schools may not be well established.

Schools are also likely to have open days, arrange visits and provide other opportunities for your child to become familiar with their new school. These activities will help your child to get to know the school and its layout, meet new teachers and understand how the school day is structured, all of which will help smooth the transition process.

WHAT CAN I DO TO MAKE SURE MY CHILD'S TRANSITION IS SUCCESSFUL?

As a parent, you can also play a very significant role in preparing your child for their transition to a new school and helping them through the sometimes difficult first few weeks as they get used to a new environment, different expectations and changes in their social world. Your child's transition to their new school will affect the whole family, and they will look to you and the other members of their family for support at this time of new beginnings in their life. You should use the time before they start their new school, and during the important first few weeks there, to make sure your child is well prepared.

When thinking about transition to a new school and what needs to happen, it's helpful to consider:

- social aspects of transition
- getting used to a new school
- motivation for learning.

The diagram opposite illustrates these three areas. Schools should address all of these areas in supporting your child and you can also help at this critical time.

> **Transition will impact on many areas of your child's life, so it is important that they are supported in all of these if they are to be ready to make the most of the new opportunities available to them.**

Social aspects of transition

Moving to a new, almost inevitably larger, school will have a significant social impact on children. There will be lots of opportunities for your child to make new friends – how much they do so will help you gauge how successful their transition is likely to be.

You can support your child by encouraging them to make new friendships. Support your child by letting them know that they can talk to you about anything that is concerning them. Talk to them about how they can go about making new friends and about the new friends they have made, if they are willing to do this, but don't be too insistent if they are reluctant to talk about friendships. In this way, you will get a better idea of what's going on both at school and outside school.

Encouraging your child to take part in new activities during the summer break is another way for them to start to make new friendships. Also encourage them to join clubs and engage in other activities when they start their new school.

Getting used to a new school

Schools themselves should play a considerable role in helping your child become familiar with their new school, but you may also want to take the opportunity to visit the school with your child to get a better idea about its structure and organisation – and perhaps meet their new teacher(s).

The school day at primary school is much simpler, with classes often staying together most of the time. In contrast, your child will be moving into a far more fluid environment, where they will need to become comfortable with moving between classes with different teachers and working with different groups of their peers for different subjects.

It can be valuable preparation before starting secondary school to help your child be flexible by getting them to switch between activities fairly regularly – at least every hour, which roughly corresponds to the length of lessons in most schools.

Also spend some time making sure that they understand the expectations their new school will have of them and that they understand their timetable.

You should also talk to them about practical aspects of their new school, such as how they are going to get there and their increased independence.

Motivation for learning

Children's motivation can be affected by the changes in environment, structure and uncertainty about what's expected of them.

Schools should support children in understanding how learning will change, but parents also play a vital role here. They can motivate children by taking an interest in the subjects they're learning, thus sharing their learning journey.

The amount and nature of homework will also change, so your child may look to you for guidance. Helping them structure the time they spend on homework and other activities is one way in which you can help, as will ensuring that they have the right environment in which to study. You may also find yourself supporting their learning, particularly when they find subjects challenging.

APPENDIX

- Verbal Reasoning question types
- Non-Verbal Reasoning question types

CRACKING CODES

Crack the Number Code

Three of these four words are given in code.
The codes are **not** written in the same order as the
words and one code is missing.

SELL	SALE	MATE	TEAS
6354	1422	5431	

For these questions, mark the correct answer on the
answer sheet.

Example

Find the code for the word **SALE**.

Answer

1234

Crack the Letter Code

A B C D E F G H I J K L M N O P Q R S T U V W X Y Z
The alphabet is here to help you with these
questions. You need to work out a different code for
each question. Choose the correct answer and mark
it on the answer sheet.

Example

If the code for **FOOT** is **ENNS**,
what is the code for **TOE**?

Answer

SND

Complete the Letter Series

A B C D E F G H I J K L M N O P Q R S T U V W X Y Z
The alphabet is here to help you with these
questions. Find the next letters in the series
and mark the correct answer on the answer sheet.

Example

      CQ   DQ   EP   FP   (?)

Answer

      GO

Complete the Letter Sentence

A B C D E F G H I J K L M N O P Q R S T U V W X Y Z
The alphabet is here to help you with these
questions. Find the letters that will complete the
sentence in the best way and mark the correct
answer on the answer sheet.

Example

      AB is to **CD** as **PQ** is to (?)

Answer

      RS

CREATING WORDS

Create a Compound Word

In these questions, find **two** words, **one** from each
group, that together make **one** correctly spelt word,
without changing the order of the letters. The word
from the first group always comes first. Mark **both**
words on the answer sheet.

Example

      (out   by   open)
      (bite   like   side)

Answer

      out   **side** (The word is **outside**.)

Find the Missing Letter

In these questions, the **same** letter must fit into **both** sets of brackets, to complete the word in front of the brackets and begin the word after the brackets. Find this letter and mark it on the answer sheet.

Example

mea [?] able

si [?] op

Answer

t (The four words are **meat, table, sit, top**.)

Move a Letter

In these questions, one letter can be moved from the first word to the second word, to make two new words. The letters must **not** otherwise be rearranged and **both** new words must make sense. Find the letter that moves and mark it on the answer sheet.

Example

pound   or

Answer

u (The two new words are **pond** and **our**.)

Find the Missing Three-Letter Word

In these sentences, the word in capitals has had three letters next to each other taken out. These three letters will make one correctly spelt word without changing their order. The sentence that you make must make sense. Mark the correct three-letter word on the answer sheet.

Example

The cat scratched him with his CS.

Answer

LAW (The word in capitals is **CLAWS**.)

Complete the Third Pair in the Same Way

These questions contain three pairs of words.
Find the word that completes the last pair of words
in the **same way** as the other two pairs.
Mark it on the answer sheet.

Example

(band   ban)   (song   son)
(tear   [?   ])

Answer

tea

Create Words in the Same Way

In these questions, the three words in the second
group should go together in the **same way** as the
three in the first group. Find the word that is
missing in the second group and mark it on the
answer sheet.

Example

(man   [mat]   tip)
(bug   [?   ]   dew)

Answer

bud

USING NUMBERS

Solve Letter Sums

In these questions, letters stand for numbers. Work
out the answer to each sum, then find its letter and
mark it on the answer sheet.

Example

If A = 1, B = 2, C = 3, D = 6, E = 8,
what is the answer to this sum **written as
a letter?**

A + B + C = (?)

Answer

D

Continue the Number Series

In each question, find the number that continues the series in the most sensible way and mark it on the answer sheet.

Example

2   4   6   8   (?)

Answer

10

Find the Number to Complete the Sum

In each question, find the number that will complete the sum correctly and mark it on the answer sheet.

Example

3 + 5 = 6 + [?]

Answer

2

Find the Missing Number

In these questions, the three numbers in **each** group are related in the **same way**. Find the number that completes the last group and mark it on the answer sheet.

Example

(3   [6]   9)   (2   [4]   6)
(4   [?]   12)

Answer

8

Finding Words

Find the Hidden Four-Letter Word

In these sentences, a word of **four letters** is hidden at the **end** of one word and the **beginning** of the next word. Find the pair of words that contains the hidden word and mark this answer on the answer sheet.

Example

> The film ended happily after all.

Answer

> **film ended** (The hidden word is **mend**.)

Find Words Closest in Meaning

In these questions, find **two** words, **one** from each group, that are **closest in meaning**. Mark **both** words on the answer sheet.

Example

> (office   shop   start)
> (work   begin   end)

Answer

> **start   begin**

Find Words Opposite in Meaning

In these questions, find **two** words, **one** from each group, that are **most opposite in meaning**. Mark **both** words on the answer sheet.

Example

> (morning early wake)
> (late shop dark)

Answer

> **early late**

Find the Odd Words Out

In these questions, three of the five words are related in some way. Find the **two** words that do not go with these three and mark them **both** on the answer sheet.

Example

black   mouse   red   green   hut

Answer

mouse   hut

Find the Double Meaning

In these questions, there are two pairs of words. Only one of the five possible answers will go equally well with **both** of these pairs.
Mark it on the answer sheet.

Example

(world   globe)
(soil   ground)

Answer

earth

Find the Word Link

In these questions, find the **two** words, **one** from each group, that will complete the sentence in the best way. Mark **both** words on the answer sheet.

Example

Big is to
(small   orange   colour)
as **wide** is to
(apple   red   narrow)

Answer

small   narrow

THINKING LOGICALLY

Explore the Facts

Read the following information, then find the correct answer to the question and mark it on the answer sheet.

Example

Alice, Ewa, Nick, Charlotte and David all bring packed lunches to school.

Nick, David and Charlotte all have sandwiches.

David and Alice have a biscuit.

Nick has a chocolate bar.

Ewa, Charlotte and Alice all have a piece of fruit.

Alice and Ewa have a salad.

Who has the most things for lunch?

Answer

Alice

Read the following information, then find the correct answer to the question and mark it on the answer sheet.

Example

The children in the Jones family are called Archie, Jack, Charlie, Lucy and Emily.
Lucy is 1 year younger than Charlie.
Jack and Charlie are twins.
Archie is 3 years older than Lucy.
Jack is 8 years old.
Emily is older than Charlie, but younger than Archie.

If these statements are true, only one of the sentences below **must** be true.

Which one?

A Emily is 11.

B Archie is 2 years older than Emily.

C All the children are younger than 10.

D The sum of their ages is 45.

E Archie is 10.

Answer

E

FINDING SIMILARITIES AND DIFFERENCES

Find the Odd One Out

In each of the rows below there are five figures. Find one figure in each row that is **most unlike** the other four and **mark its letter on the answer sheet**.

Example

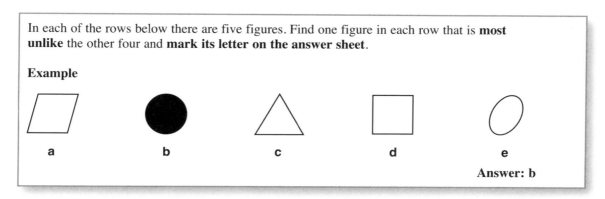

Answer: b

Find the Diagram Like the First Two

On the left of each of the rows below there are two figures that are alike. On the right there are five more figures: find which of these is most like the two figures on the left, and **mark its letter on your answer sheet**.

Example

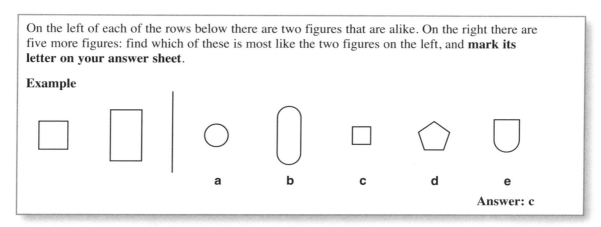

Answer: c

Find the Diagram Like the First Three

On the left of each of the rows below there are three figures that are alike. On the right there are five more figures: find which of these is most like the three figures on the left, and **mark its letter on your answer sheet**.

Example

Answer: c

COMPLETING DIAGRAMS

Complete the Series

To the left in each of the lines below there are five squares arranged in order. One of these squares has been left empty. Find which one of the five squares on the right should **take the place** of the empty square and **mark its letter on your answer sheet**.

Example

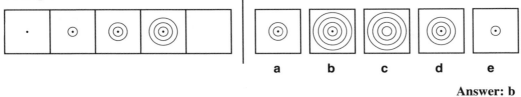

Answer: b

Complete the Grid

In the big square on the left of each line below one of the small squares has been left empty. One of the five figures on the right should fill the empty square. Find this figure and **mark its letter on your answer sheet**.

Example

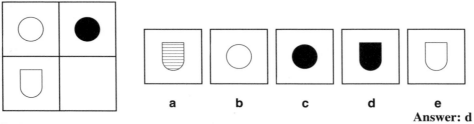

Answer: d

Complete the Pair

On the left of each of the rows below are two shapes with an arrow between them. Decide how the second is related to the first. After these there is a third shape, then an arrow and then five more shapes. Decide which of the five shapes goes with the **third** one to **make a pair** like the two on the left. **Mark its letter on your answer sheet**.

Example

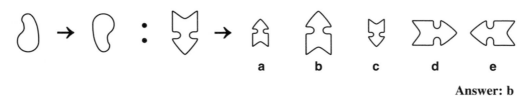

Answer: b

CRACKING CODES

Crack the Vertical Code

To answer these questions you have to work out a code. On the left are some shapes and the codes that go with them. You must decide how the code letters go with the shapes. Then find the correct code for the **test shape** from the set of five codes on the right. **Mark its letter on your answer sheet**.

Look at **Example 1**:

Answer: **b**

Crack the Horizontal Code

To answer these questions you have to work out a code. In the boxes on the left are shapes and the code letters that go with them. The top letters mean something different to the bottom ones. You must decide how the letters go with the shapes. Then find the correct code for the **test shape** from the set of five codes on the right. **Mark its letter on your answer sheet**.

Look at **Example 1**:

   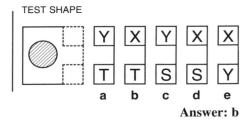

Answer: **b**